DEFLATED

Causes and Cures

of the

Great Recession

of

2009

J Duncan Smeaton

Inauguration ceremony for President Obama, January 2009.

Variation on the Benediction:

…help us work for the day when
Black stops stereotyping White….
When all Brown are legally 'round ….
When Yellow and Red are terms long forgotten…
And when White gets kudos for doing right…

Let all those not inclined to steal from others in the name of compassion, bailout, or social justice
Say you bet…
Say you bet..
And you bet.

Word play aside, what a great day.

Contents

Foreword

The prime cause of this Great Recession was the high price of oil. The price of oil is not something that governments can control; it is a result of the level of world economic activity. Only in the long run can governments reduce our dependence on oil and as a result reduce the upward pressure on the price of oil.

An equally important cause of this Great Recession was the anti-inflationary monetary policy of the last decade. Insufficient money in the economy choked growth, all in the name of fighting future inflation. The money supply is controlled by the government.

There was no asset "bubble". Real estate, and other, prices were not frothy, and did not trigger the recession.

The subprime panic was brought about by an overly restrictive monetary policy; the underlying assets, on average, were and are sound.

In the spirit of scientific enquiry, I suggest that what I propose in this book should be treated as a theory subject to disproof by argument and fact. I find no facts to disprove my arguments but such facts may yet arise.

Let me summarize my suggestions for a way forward for America.

1. BUY OIL.

Fill up your strategic reserves chock-a-block full. Use government tax wedges to cause private industry to fill up all available private storage facilities with oil. Buy, or encourage American businesses to buy, tankers on the open ocean and fill them with purchased oil. Encourage, via tax incentives, Americans to take equity positions in oil companies that have solid claims on reserves throughout the world. And, perhaps radically, have the Federal Reserve infuse cash into the economy by buying up oil derivatives, hedges, calls, etc, up to and perhaps beyond a price of $60 bbl.

(This book was written in Feb 09 when oil was $45 bbl. The economy can adjust to any price of oil given time. It is the <u>shock</u> of quickly rising prices that causes the problem. Oil price shock causes recessions; high oil price lowers the standard of living. As of Oct 09, oil has hit $80 in a short period of time – a bad sign).

2. Liquidize the economy.

Blast through the Keynesian liquidity trap. Have the Federal Reserve banks buy up, from the commercial banks, all senior paper it can find. Even go so far as to mandate that if the Feds want to buy an asset from a bank, the bank has to sell. In time the banks will be so cash rich and asset poor that they will have to start lending – and they are the best institutions to figure out where and where not to lend money. The government should not be buying damaged assets, it should be buying quality assets (possible exception: sub-prime derivatives) and pumping cash into the economy until such time as there is strong evidence that inflation is growing.

3. Treat fiscal stimulus with GREAT CAUTION.

Apart from the pork barrelling, and skimming, that is always associated with this kind of spending, there is a far more dangerous aspect. Massive public spending shifts resources away from where the jobs are to totally new areas and often new people. This can cause a massive structural shift. The recovery, once it shifts back to traditional needs such as transportation (cars), household capital (washing machines), will find that the core of American industry has been shut down – inflation will surely follow a difficult restart, and an even greater shifting of the core economy to offshore will result.

Before we jump into the argument behind these suggestions, let me offer the following overall opinion. This downturn is not the result of a bubble or an irrational burst of positive economic activity, but rather, this downturn itself represents a negative bubble; an irrational burst of negative economic activity. Let me give you a taste of the argument by the following example: I am looking at a report from a senior economist from the Wharton School who is agonizing over the bloated state of house prices in recent years. He implies that the peak average US house price of $225,000 was bloated, unsustainable and one of the key causes of the Recession. Excuse me?! An average price which is below replacement cost?! An average price a mere four times family income (2007 median family income > $50,000)?! On a key asset, long lived, placed on that irreplaceable asset, land?! Bloated? Over-priced? No! And that was at the peak!

Causes and Cures

We are deflated. And deflating.

The business psyche is deflated, and deflating. GNP is deflated, and deflating. Oil is deflated, and deflating. House prices are deflated, and deflating. And most ominous, overall prices are deflated, and deflating.

This could be the Great Deflation. And deflation is much more difficult to defeat than inflation.

What caused this state of affairs? And what to do about it?

There are many opinions on the cause of the Great Recession of 09. There many opinions on what to do about it.

Let us start with the causes. Below is a list of those most mentioned in the media. What do you think is the key one?

1. High oil prices?
2. The Sub-Prime Collapse?
3. The Bubble in real estate prices?
4. A frothy stock market?
5. The Deficit – Internal?
6. The Deficit- External?
7. Globalization?
8. Faux-Inflation fighting?
9. Greed?
10. Lack of Regulation?
11. Incompetence?
12. Unions?
13. A borrow-to-buy mentality?
14. All of the Above?
15. Some of the Above?

The winner, hands down, is number one: High oil prices.

What will lead to the Great Recovery of 09/10?

1. Low oil prices?
2. Lenders lending?

3. Rising real estate prices?
4. A ten thousand Dow, or thereabouts?
5. A serious reduction of the fiscal deficit, or better: a reduction of the fiscal debt?
6. A serious reduction of the external deficit and debt?
7. Policy encouragement of made-in-America?
8. Attacking deflation?
9. Policy encouragement of religion not Mammon?
10. Pervasive regulation of key sectors of the economy – finance in particular?
11. Extend government support for Universities?
12. Apply anti-trust laws to unions as well as corporations?
13. Campaign for save-to-buy mentality?
14. All of the above?
15. Some of the above?

For good measure, let us consider as well:

16. Extend the sector-specific and company-specific bailout program?
17. Implement Keynesian fiscal stimulus i.e. expand the deficit?
18. Implement Galbraithian fiscal stimulus i.e. infrastructure: roads, parks, health care…?
19. Fix the money supply at a constant growth rate and let the economy self-solve a la Friedman?
20. Lower interest rates further?
21. Expand the Feds liquidization program – buy senior paper?

The winner, hands down, again, number one: Low oil prices.

But there are some policies which we should avoid, and some we should encourage, to speed along the recovery process. Liquidization, number twenty one, is my favourite recovery policy.

A brief preliminary note: The bars in all the graphs in this book represent Recessions. As there is no official definition of a Recession, I have used the NBER (National Bureau of Economic Research) peak-to-trough contraction as a proxy. All the data represented in graph form is sourced from FRED unless otherwise noted. Thank you to FRED (Federal Reserve Economic Data) and his founders at the St Louis Fed: user friendly and comprehensive.

We begin by considering the supposed causes in the order listed above.

First, oil.

High Oil Prices

Common sense will take us a long way on this one.

Energy is required to transport people, and goods. Growing demographics, and growing consumption from growing world incomes, suggest that ever growing amounts of energy are needed. If the transport of people, and/or goods falls off that is reflected in a decline in GDP (Gross Domestic Product - a measure of overall economic activity). Increasing the cost of this all important component causes a constriction of demand.

Energy use in the productive process is pervasive. Not only is energy required to transform one type of material to another e.g. silica to glass, but it is needed at every step of the assembly process including shaping, cutting, milling, forming, trimming etc. Although much of this is done by electricity, all energy forms are substitutes and increased cost of oil causes increased use of substitutes such as electricity and a subsequent upward push on the price of these substitutes. This in turn pushes prices of the end goods higher and causes overall constriction of demand i.e. lower GDP.

Of course oil is the main source of energy as it remains one of the most efficient means of transporting energy from its source e.g. under ground, to where it is used e.g. engine cylinder.

Consider what had happened to the price of this all important part of GDP: it had risen in price from $30 to $144, staying above $100 for months. This price increase occurred over the last five years! Even if the economy had been able to pass on these price increases to the end products in a timely and efficient manner so we could have adjusted to less energy-using consumption, the result would have shown up in a pure cost increase overall i.e. inflation. That in turn would have been 'corrected' by high interest rates and a concomitant slowing of the economy.

High prices transfers purchasing power to the suppliers of oil. If these recipients bought the same products that suffered the cost increases then there would be little impact beyond a shifting of resources from one group to another. However, citizens of the Middle East have different spending patterns from the average American. Either they hoard the resources (causes American deflation), or they use it for geopolitical purposes, or, no less troublesome, they cause structural shifts by purchasing a different set of consumption goods. In the long run it washes out – we have some winners and some losers. Unfortunately, we live in the short run: the structural shifting of the economy causes deflation and constriction of production.

Here is a sobering thought: Assume that for every dollar spent, on anything, a portion of that dollar is in turn spent on energy. A reasonable assumption! But consider the non-energy part: the assumption still applies i.e. a portion spent on the residual still has a portion of it spent on energy. The result?: in limit, a dollar spent on anything, is a dollar spent on energy. Not only that! Assume that for every dollar spent on energy, a fraction of the proceeds is spent on oil. So, again in limit, a dollar spent on anything means a dollar spent on oil. By this reasoning, and under the key assumption, $32,565 spent on a Chevy Malibu means that $32,565 is spent on oil. Comments?

So where does all this common sense take us? Oil is critically important to the economy. As oil had tripled in price over the last five years, and because producers were not able to pass on prices quickly, profits and confidence fell. The economy suffered a structural shock, and slowed down i.e. GNP fell.

The evidence from the historical data is very pronounced. A significant jump in oil prices predated every recession since 1970. The only exception, the recession of 1983, can be interpreted as an aftershock (price of oil did not correct, therefore...) of the huge price increase of two years earlier. I have taken the series of monthly oil prices and divided by the CPI (Consumer Price Index) for non-energy items, to get a 'real' cost index of oil. The plot of this series is shown in the following diagrams together with an indication of the recession years. The result?: spiking oil prices – recession; flat or falling oil prices - no recession, even recovery.

The steady sharp rise over the past decade is particularly unique and troublesome: The Great Recession of 09 may be deeper and longer than past recessions.

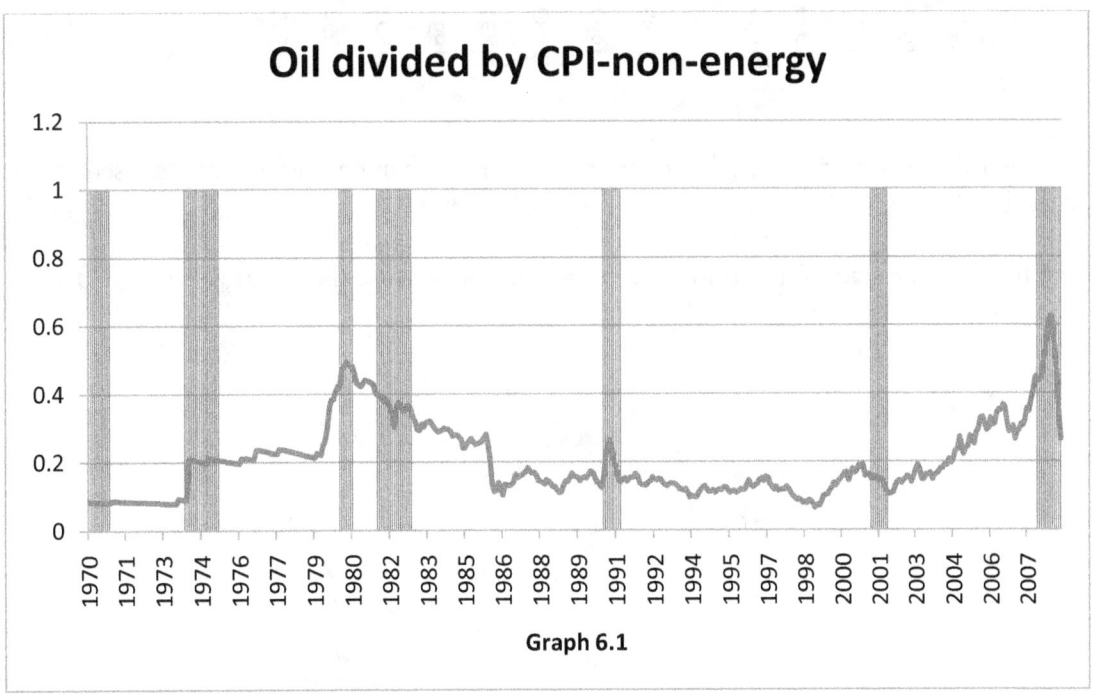

Graph 6.1

In graph 6.1, the price of oil has been divided by the corresponding CPI (Consumer Price Index non-energy) to show the 'real' price of oil over the period 1970 to the present. Clearly, oil price spikes lead to recessions – and oil price drops lead to recovery.

In graph 7.1, the price of all energy (CPI – energy only) has been divided by the corresponding non-energy CPI. Again, in the modern period, rising energy costs lead to recessions. This is even more pronounced than when only oil price was considered. In the pre 1970 period, there is no evidence of this recession / energy cost relationship.

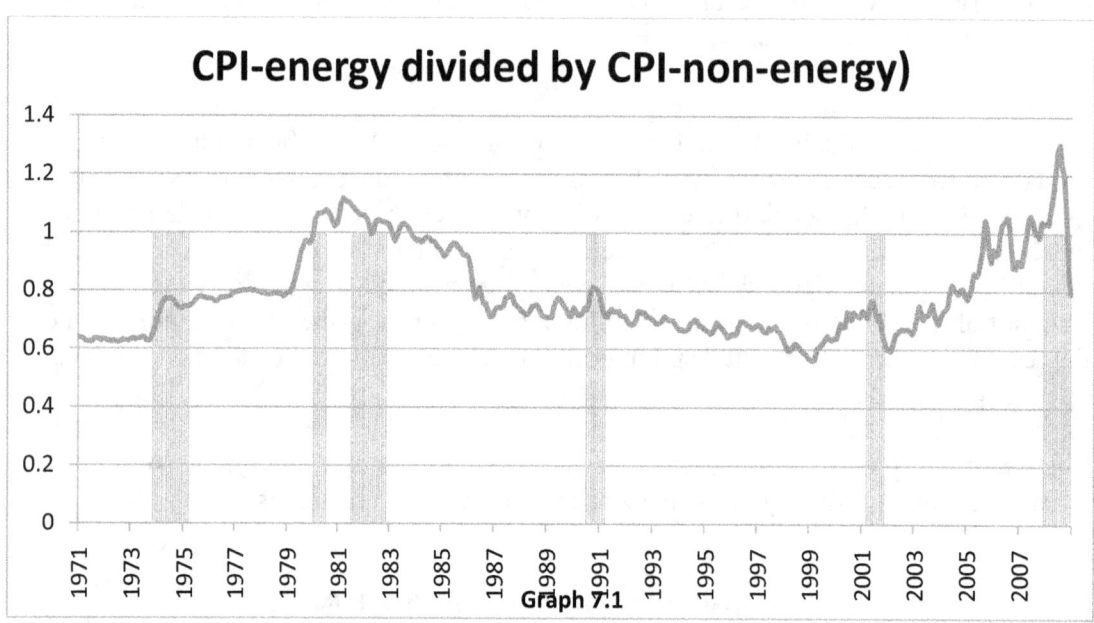

CPI-energy divided by CPI-non-energy)

Graph 7.1

So high oil prices predated each modern recession, and can be said to have 'caused' these recessions.

Can the same be said of the sub-prime collapse? Did it cause the Great Recession? Did it cause any of the other recessions?

Asset Bubbles

The Sub-Prime Collapse

The root cause of the current financial panic is the collapse in value of the mortgage backed securities of Freddie Mac (Federal Home Loan Mortgage Corporation) and Fanny Mae (Federal National Mortgage Association). Whether or not this panic is warranted is another issue. But panic there is. Assigning blame for this situation is fairly straightforward: the Clinton administration, in 1995, began assigning credit to these two institutions (affordable housing credit) in exchange for their buying and packaging sub-prime securities. The Bush administration in 2003 tried valiantly, twice, to enact reforms to address the looming valuation problem but was blocked by the Senate Committee on Banking Housing and Urban Affairs. This committee let us be kind, seemed to reflect the narrow interests of those institutions it was 'regulating' (oversight responsibilities).

Fanny Mae was spun off in 1968 from a federal government department with a mandate to bundle real estate backed mortgages into securities which could be marketed in their own right. Freddie Mac was set up in 1970 by a Congressional Act to perform the same function and to give the market some 'competition'. It is estimated that these two institutions have approximately $5 trillion placed in the market. Both institutions are heavily regulated private institutions whose assets have NO government guarantee as to their value. It has always puzzled me how the rate of return on these combination securities could be higher than the rate of return of their component securities. Of course the answer, now evident, lies in the fact that higher return sub-prime paper was bundled in with the quality stuff. The result of this risk orientation is obvious for all to see.

Background:

The Community Reinvestment Act of 1977 was intended to address the problem of 'redlining' by which financial institutions in effect blacklisted entire geographical regions as being un-credit-worthy. The teeth of the Bill lay in the provisions for approval of new bank branches, and for mergers and acquisitions. Such approvals were subject to consideration of the banks discriminatory credit practices against low income neighbourhoods. The Act applied to all banks operating under the Federal Deposit Insurance arrangement. The Act did not require these banks to make unsound loans although it certainly pushed them to make loans they otherwise would not make.

The CRA Act was further strengthened under the Clinton administration through the Riegle-Neal Act of 1994. Under this legislation, CRA ratings were made a consideration for applicants for interstate branches.

Again the Act was strengthened by President Clinton in 1995 by legislation directed towards reforming the CRA to be more consistent and to clarify performance standards. At this time, CRA ratings were made public. As Robert Rubin, Assistant to the President for Economic Policy, said at the time: "…this is consistent with the strategy to deal with inner city and distressed rural communities".

President Clinton's Office of the Comptroller of the Currency was directed to allow CRA subjected lending to claim community development loan credits for loans made to help finance environmental cleanup or redevelopment of industrial sites.

The Gramm-Leach-Beley Act repealed that part of the Glass-Steagall Act (the Bank Act of 1933) that prohibited banks from offering a full range of credit services. President Clinton described this Act as expanding the CRA.

On the other hand, beginning in 2005, the Office of Thrift Supervision allowed thrifts with capitalization greater than $1B to avoid certain CRA obligations.

Some argue that because the Acts enacted under President Clinton were done with a Republican Congress, they were an exercise in deregulation by the Right which caused subprime gambling. Yet it was all done under President Clinton's watch and with his encouragement, and certainly no veto was attempted. A reasonable interpretation of the Gramm-Leach-Beley Act was that it was intended to strengthen the CRA and had the unintended consequence of expanding the subprime market.

It is important to note that the Thrifts and Banks were at no time required to make unsound loans. That so many loans turned out to be unsound can be laid at the feet of the 'surprise' of rocketing oil prices, and the bias towards risk taking of these institutions.

The odd part of all this is that the very people who caused the mess (albeit for some good intentions) are the same people in charge of fixing it. Some good old fashioned firings might be in order. Certainly the inherent conflict of mixing social policy with prudent financial oversight should be reviewed. It would appear, once again, that the regulatee has ended up controlling the regulator.

If the Bush revisions had been implemented, and if oil prices had not discombobulated the economy, there would be no Panic, and no Great Recession. In any case, I suspect most of these asset backed securities are sound. It is important to minimize the ability of those who took out these mortgages to walk away from them. Best way to do that is to liquidize the economy and cause underlying asset values to rise relative to the currency. Lots of money means less value to money and more value to assets.

The sub-prime crisis arose because mortgages were issued to borrowers with little regard to traditional tests of ability to re-pay such as asset base of the borrower, or free income stream of the borrower. Furthermore, these 'weak' mortgages albeit with high interest rates, were bundled with other, somewhat stronger paper, and marketed as high quality derivatives. These mortgages are referred to as sub-prime because the quality of asset that is mortgaged is under, or sub, the quality of assets that can be used to obtain near–prime interest. Crummy houses, and impoverished borrowers, are associated with sub-prime quality mortgages.

Why were mortgages issued under these conditions? It is trite to say it was based on greed. We are all greedy. To lay the blame on lack of proper regulation is inappropriate: the process was started deliberately under the watchful and knowledgeable eyes of the Clinton administration and the Feds Greenspan. Why?: to encourage renters to become owners. Not a bad objective for all sorts of personal and societal reasons.

Could it have worked? You bet! If the underlying asset prices had held or grown, and if borrower incomes had been secure or grown, there would have been no sub-prime mess. In normal times, the policy may have worked. Two things went wrong: borrowers and lenders were not held fiscally responsible i.e. they could escape the consequences of bad judgement (bankruptcies, bailouts etc), and an oil-driven recession was underway.

Had those institutions and persons responsible for the bad judgement on the economy been held fully responsible, the system would have self-corrected at a much earlier stage; fewer and fewer sub-prime mortgages would have been issued. The problem wasn't lack of regulation but rather enforcement of the basic laws of private property and debt obligation.

As to solving such crises by regulation: Beware. The regulator always always always ends up being controlled by the regulatee. Always! Educate, don't regulate!

But what about the value of those underlying assets? Were they really over-priced? Was it a 'frothy' market? Was it an investment 'bubble'?

The Bubble in real estate prices

The collapse of asset values, in particular of the value of private residences: did that cause the recession? Were these assets significantly overpriced?

No!

There are two factors which suggest that residential real estate is not now overpriced nor was it overpriced before the sub-prime crisis. Certainly there are and were pockets of overbuild and over-valuation. But consider:

1. Average square footage of a primary residence (new) is just over 2,500 sq ft (source: DOE). Average cost for new construction ranges from $80 to $200 – average $118 (source B4UBUILD). Therefore, the average replacement cost for a primary residence is approx $300,000. This means that current house prices, and even prices before the Recession, are well under replacement costs. This puts no value on the land. In some locales, suffering temporary economic downturns because of layoffs in one or two key industries, the house prices are less than one quarter of replacement value. In San Diego, one of the most ideal living, and working (normal times) areas of the country, $300,000 will buy you a view home

in a very nice neighbourhood. Hardly the stuff of a 'bubble' in asset values. The South Sea 'Bubble' was an 'internet bust on steroids' at a time when information was hard to come by. The Dutch tulip craze involved valuations many multiples of cost. A difficult concept: defining tulips as an asset in any case.

2. House prices as a multiple of family income are sitting at around two. That is: two times average family income will buy you an average house. Hardly extravagant considering the house is a primary mode of living, and that with basic maintenance is a long lived asset. And very little new land is being produced. In my city, historically, anything fewer than four is a 'buy' and anything over six suggests caution.

Considering that in-migration continues, and that there are more newborns than deaths, to have land valued at zero or less is an aberration. Add to that the fact that interest rates are near zero and can be locked in for a long time, makes such a long term asset even more attractive. As to the banks unwillingness to lend: patience. As argued below, the only policy worth pursuing to wind up the Great Recession is for the Feds to liquidize bank assets so that sooner or later they will lend to survive.

But what about other non-real estate prices: had they been frothy?

A Frothy Stock market

The Dow

Something to give us pause for thought:

In August 1929, the DOW stood at 380. A year later it was down 37% to 240. Over the next year it dropped a further 42%, and in the third year it fell a further 47% to 73. Seven month later, March 1933 it bottomed out at 55, a full 86% off the level of 1929. It took until 1954 to reach the peak level of 1929. The current DOW, at approximately 8,000, is 43% off the peak of 13,930 reached in Oct 2007 (using raw monthly DOW Industrials). If it were to drop as in the early years of the Depression, it would bottom out at 1,950 sometime in 2012, and would not reach the 2007 peak until 2032!

In the following two graphs, 12.1 and 12.2, the raw DOW industrial average has been plotted.

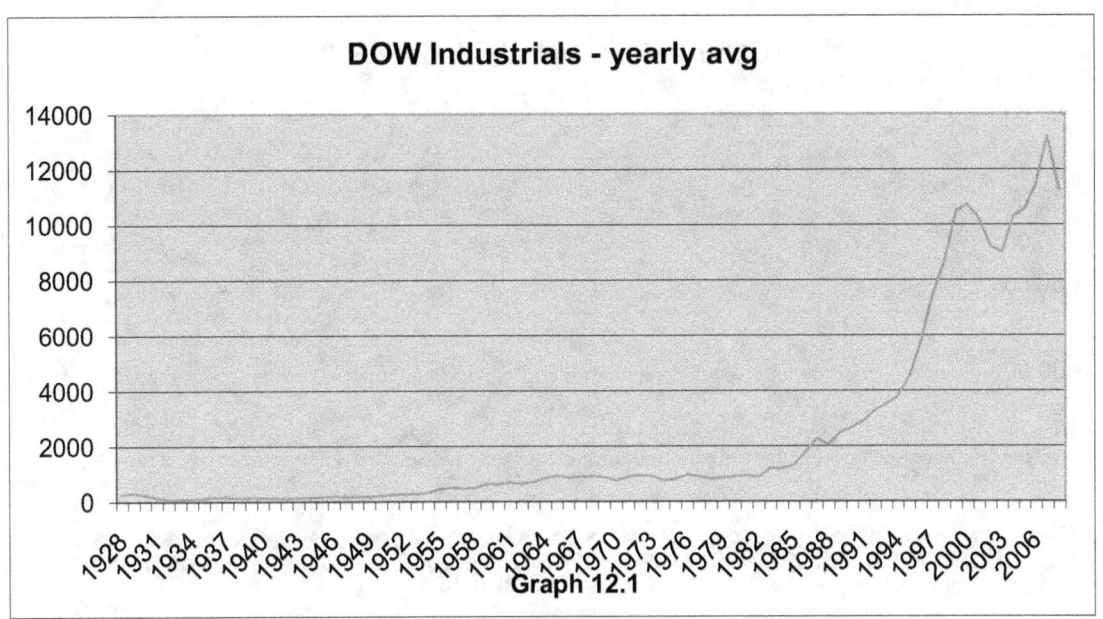

DOW Industrials - yearly avg

Graph 12.1

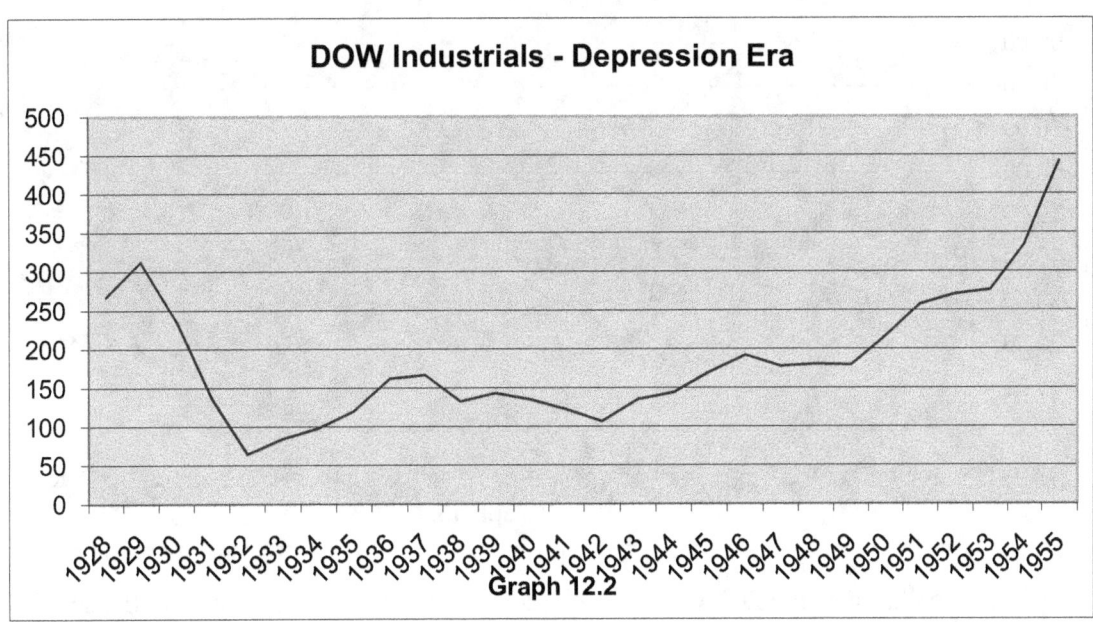

DOW Industrials - Depression Era

Graph 12.2

Let us consider a different look at the DOW. Monthly data <u>adjusted for inflation</u> of the DOW Industrial average, as shown in graphs 13.1 and 13.2, show the index to have been well above trend in recent years. But what trend? During this recent period, PE ratios were not unduly high, being in the mid-teens for senior equity such as found in the DOW average; compare these PE's with those stratospheric values associated with the Internet bubble of the late nineties.

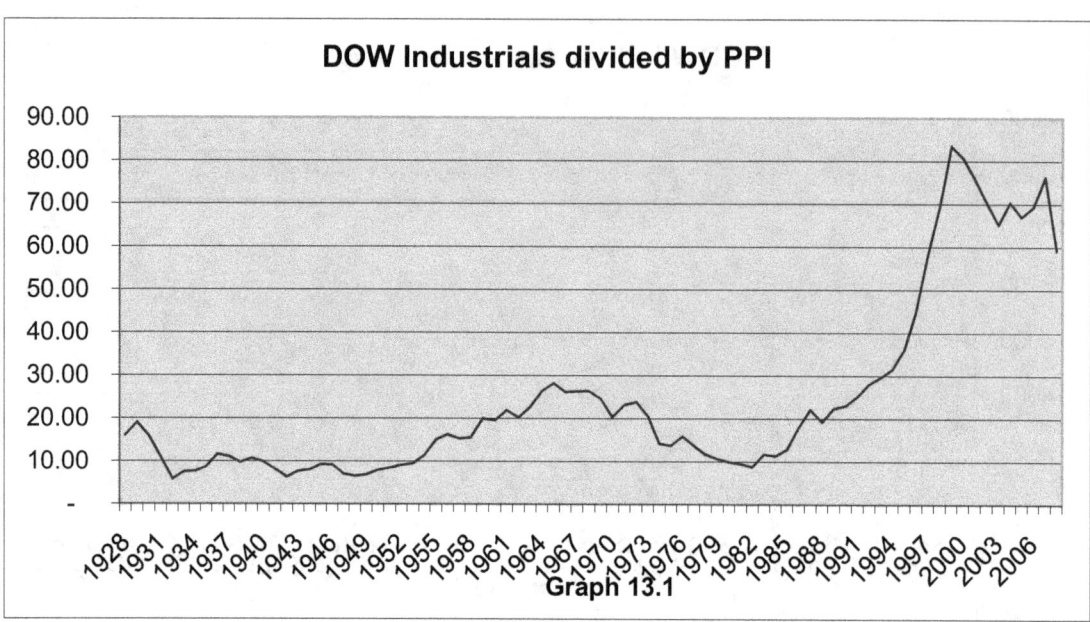

Graph 13.1

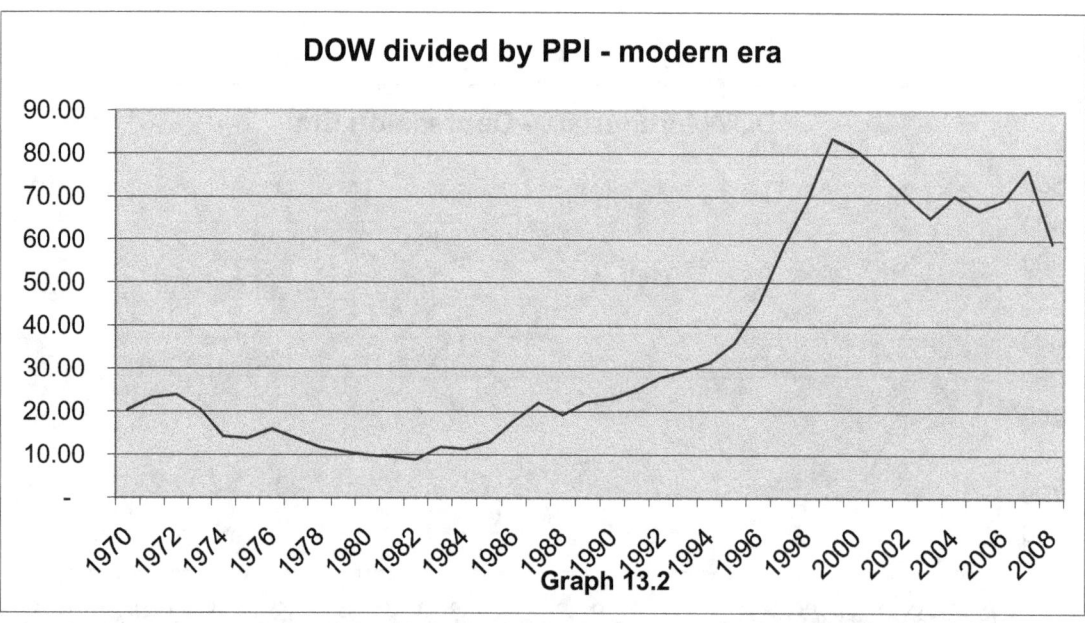

Graph 13.2

The current collapse of the DOW could well have been nothing more than a collapse of future earnings potential of underlying equities, which in turn reflected the spreading of the effects of high oil prices.

There are two fundamentally opposing views of the stock market valuations. Some, such as John Maynard Keynes, the 'great' economist of the thirties, argue that the market is irrational and reflects the fears and foibles and greed of the average investor. In this view, the DOW should be taken as an indicator of nothing of substance. Others view the market as being the average of all the best forecasts and is in that sense totally rational. This latter view is not incompatible with the 'random walk' view of stock prices, but it does imply that the art of forecasting is a random walk.

Page | 13

Neither of these views of stock valuations would lead us to the conclusion that the 'frothy' market of the last five years was a cause of the current problems. The DOW at any time could go in either direction, according to the irrational view. The rationalist view holds that, even at its peak, the DOW simply reflected the then current view of the future. Neither would lead us to think that the DOW was 'too' high, and would 'crash' as in 1929.

But the trend is there and it warrants a little consideration. Let us turn to graph 13.1. To my eye, it looks like there was a solid uptrend after WWII, lasting until 1965, which may have reflected the rolling out of all the technological innovations from the war years and embedded in a relatively new capital set (factories had to be retooled after the war). The downtrend after the mid-sixties to the early eighties may have reflected the loss of competitive edge to foreign producers, Japan, and China in particular. High and growing oil prices over the early part of this period didn't help. The trend from the early eighties to the early nineties, good solid growth, coincides with the rollout of cheap and ubiquitous computing power. The accelerated trend that followed coincides with the internet boom and the subsequent collapse aligns with the more sober assessment of internet companies with PE ratios in the hundreds.

All very interesting but it is worth reminding ourselves that after the fact rationalization of the data is not scientific. The scientific method requires that one first make predictions then use the historical data to see if the theory is disproved; only then can one regard the theory as valid subject to further 'disproof'. Strictly: a theory is not proven but rather it is not disproved. Our little musing on the DOW (after adjusted by the PPI) was definitely not scientific. Fun, but not much use.

My reading of the chicken bones: the current DOW (in the 6,000 – 8,000) range is well under long term trend. Furthermore, a DOW of 14,000 or thereabouts was not so frothy as to trigger massive pullbacks, in and of itself.

The DOW equities, and indeed all equities, represent wealth holdings for many Americans. When the value of these equities collapses, it has a major impact on consumption. Without corrective measures the consequent shrinkage in consumption can lead to recession. But the drop in the DOW is not a prime mover. Something had to trigger the change in expectations reflected in these equities. It is that something we are searching for. So far, high and rising oil prices seems to be the most logical explanation.

We now consider deficits, internal and external, and ask if they could have been the key drivers behind the Great Recession of 09.

Deficits

The Great Deficit

There is no 'great' deficit. Deficits have been with us for a long time. They are pervasive and not in and of themselves recession causing. The series of graphs labelled 16.1 through 17.2, tell the story. There is no direct association between deficits and recessions except when the effects of inflation and population growth are removed. There is no abnormal change in the deficit in recent years. There is some evidence that deficits increase after a recession; a likely consequence of tax shortfalls and of fiscal stimulus.

Consider how deficits are funded. They are funded by issuing government debt (Treasury Bills, Bonds etc). Who buys this debt?: ultimately the public. It may be indirect: Reserve Banks can buy debt with newly created money but this either causes inflation (and so the public pays) or it reduces deflation (again the public pays but now it is seen as correcting a problem). The point here is that the public in effect buys the debt. A deficit doesn't cause all of the public to go in hock but rather one part of the public goes in hock to another part of the public. Nothing wrong with this as long as all parties are willing. Ah, but there's the rub. Government spending is basically one segment of the population benefiting from monies taken from all segments of the population. Theft, if you will. If the monies are collected as taxes then it is pay as you go. The reason deficits are in such disrepute is not because they cause recessions, but because one part of the public becomes indebted to another part, involuntarily, and without necessarily receiving the benefits.

However, given that government spending is necessary/good for some things, then debt can be a reasonable way of funding this spending (if future benefits exceed current costs).

So deficit spending causes winners and losers within the society. It only causes a net loss in the sense that it is involuntary. This goes to the core of the justification for any government spending. But is does not cause recessions. And it certainly did not cause the Great Recession of 09.

Of course if the debt issued by the government is taken up by foreigners then there are other issues at stake.

Graph 16.1, below, shows the Surplus (Deficit) adjusted for inflation and adjusted for population growth. Unlike in graphs 16.2 through 17.2, we see an increase in this adjusted deficit before each of the modern recessions. This likely reflects the unexpected cost increases from high oil prices burdening government operations (going over budget because of oil).

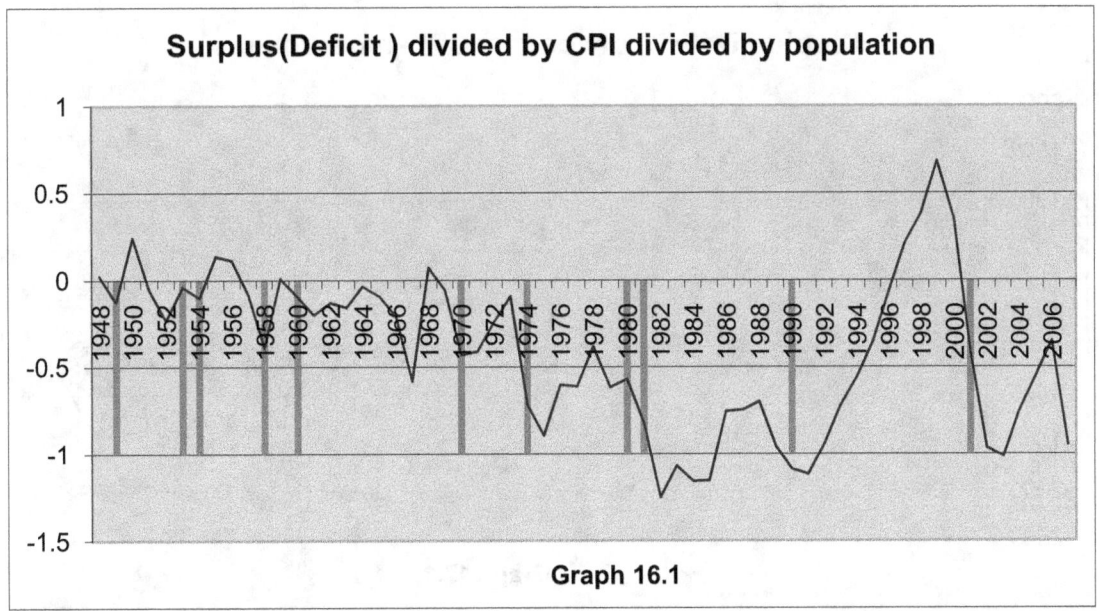

Graph 15.2 shows inflation adjusted surplus/deficit over the long span - since 1913.

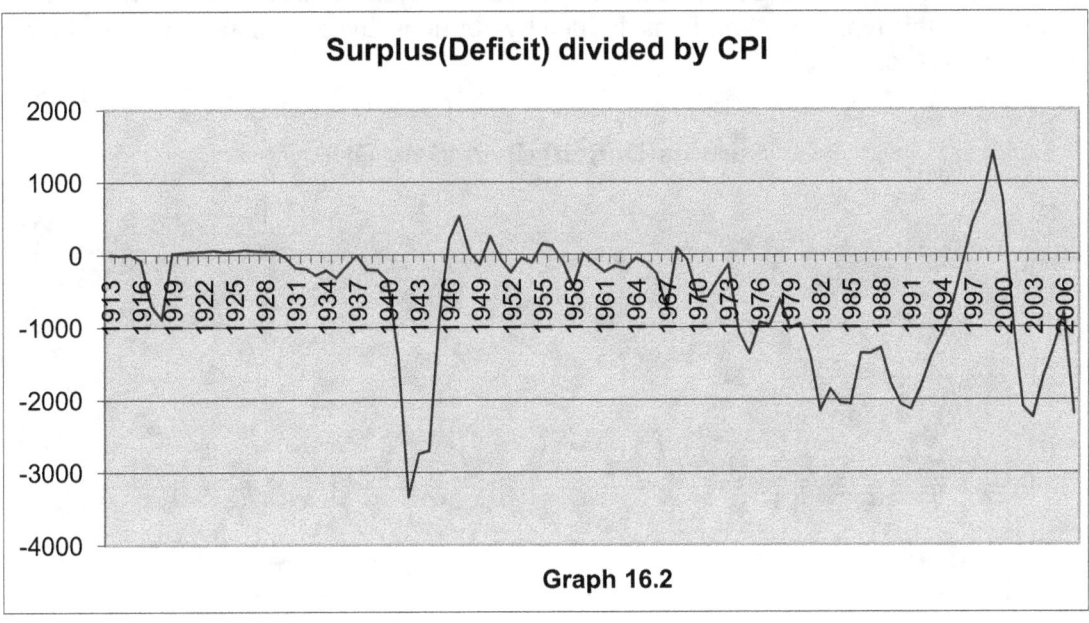

Graph 17.1 shows inflation adjusted surplus/deficit in the modern era; no evident correlation to recessions.

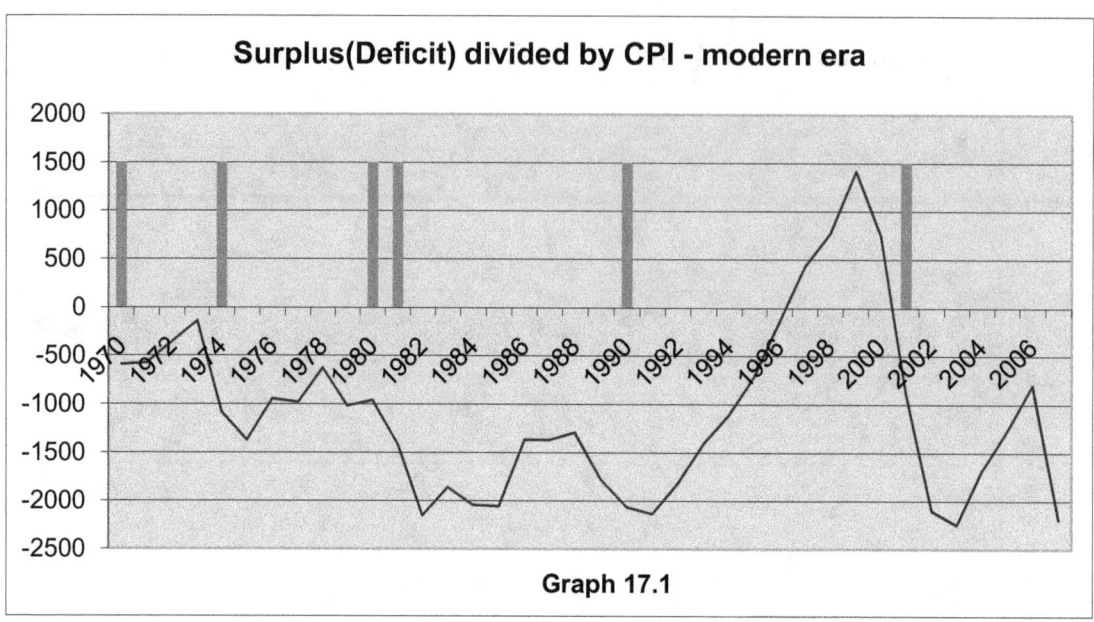

Graph 17.1

Graph 17.2 shows surplus/deficit relative to Gross National Product. Nothing abnormal there. Note: this represents $millions divided by $billions; the percentage range is plus 5% to minus 6%.

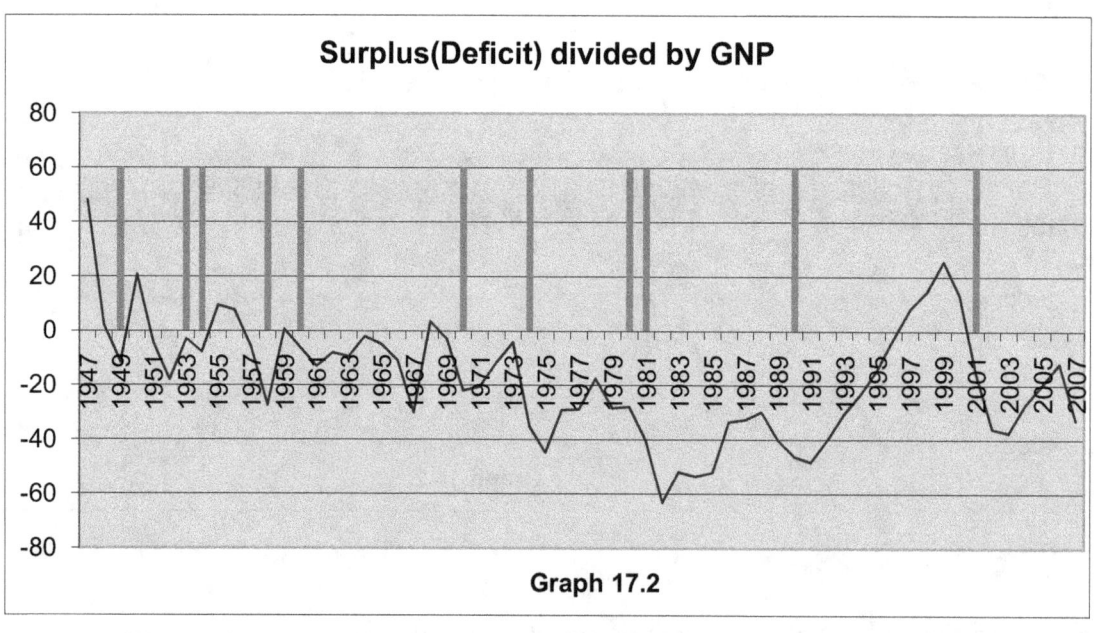

Graph 17.2

Foreign Debt

As the graphs labelled 18.1 through 19.1 clearly show there is no causal relationship to recessions found in the recent balance of payments data. The balance of trade (Exports minus imports) is the yin to the yang of capital flows. A surplus, or positive, trade balance of trade is offset by a net outflow of capital (investment) to foreigners. A negative trade balance (as is the case since 1990 and before) is balanced by a net inflow of investment i.e. foreigners are buying our debt instruments. Therefore, these graphs show the degree to which America is growing its foreign indebtedness.

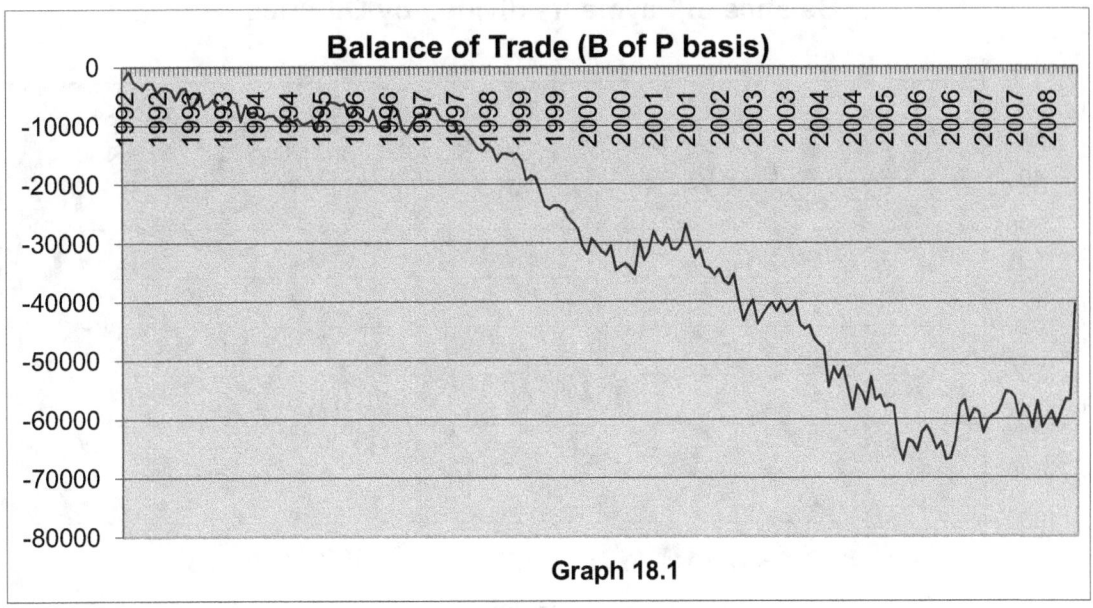

Graph 18.1

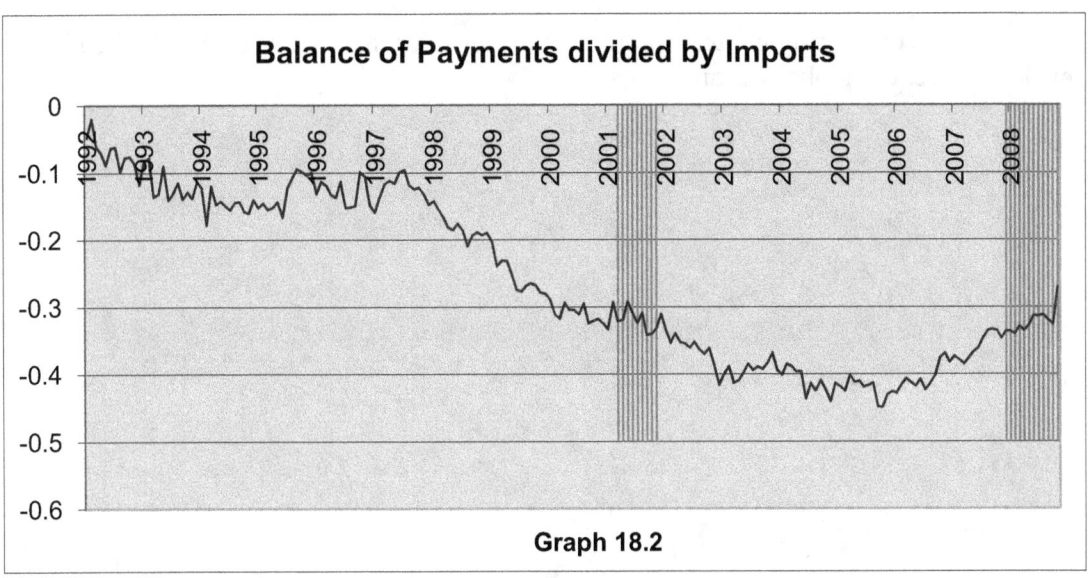

Graph 18.2

This next graph, 19.1, shows that once the effect of oil is taken away from the trade balance, the balance on current account would have improved. This would suggest that the external deficit, and growing indebtedness to foreigners, is tied up with the price of oil. Only in this indirect sense can it be said that external indebtedness is associated with recessions. In and of itself external indebtedness does not cause recessions.

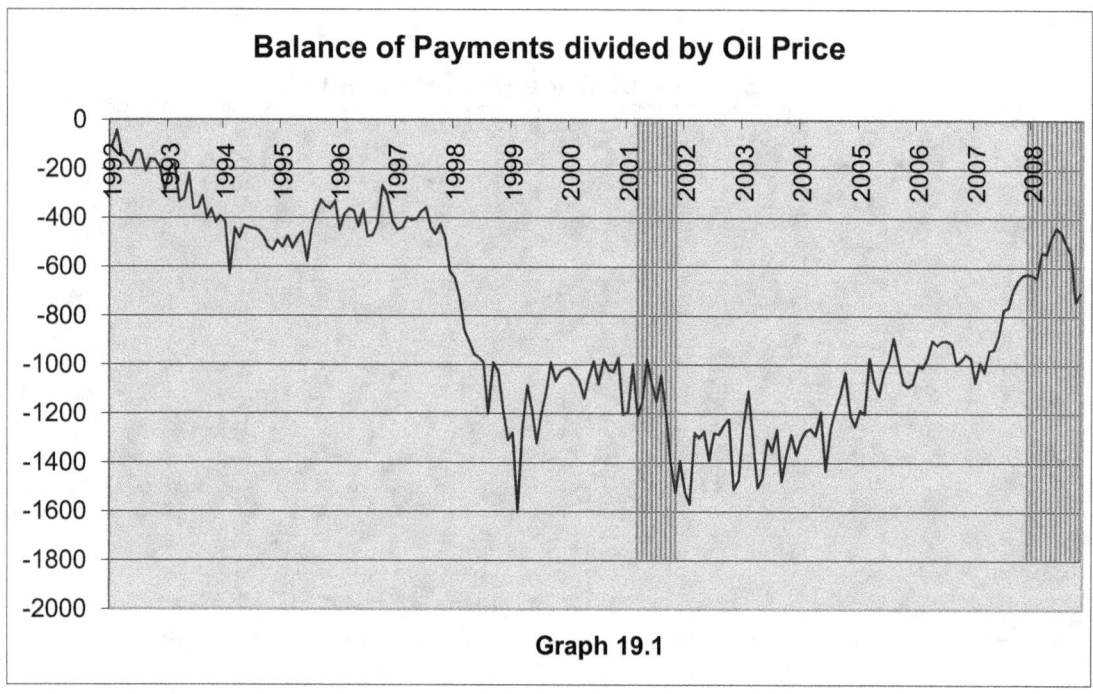

Balance of Payments divided by Oil Price

Graph 19.1

While we are considering matters foreign, let us consider that evil so often attacked in this latest election: globalization.

Globalization

Protectionism didn't cause this recession, but protectionism could deepen it.

If you find yourself faltering in your belief that free and freer trade is good for all, go immediately to Adam Smith's 'The Wealth of Nations', and read the first hundred pages.

Consider this:

It is generally acknowledged that while the Smoot-Hawley Tariff Act of 1930 (and the nonsense that led up to it) may or may not have been a prime cause of the Depression, it certainly exacerbated it and prolonged it. That was at a time when imports were roughly 4% of GNP. Now, with imports in excess of 14% of GNP, a similar protectionist reaction might have an even greater impact.

In Canada you find a constant stream of talk, from vested interests, about the evils of free trade (globalization is the term of choice as it sounds a bit sinister). They suggest that Canada loses and America wins – a zero sum game at best – from free trade. In America you find the same type of argument, often from related interests, arguing just the opposite. They can't be both right! In fact, they are both wrong. Trade increases and GNP/capita increases wherever there is free trade. Certainly there can be temporary losers, in particular those industries that are artificially sheltered by 'regulation' or unfair market constraints.

It also follows that if constriction of trade through protectionist policies causes less income and less wealth than the status quo, then freer trade will create wealth and incomes relative to the status quo. In these times America should be breaking down barriers, getting on with GATT, welcoming free trade with Columbia, breaking down the barriers v.v. Canada.

We might also remind ourselves of the Theory of Comparative Advantage. It holds that countries will specialize in what they do relatively best and import that which they do relatively less well. This holds even when one country does everything better than another country. In other words, everyone produces and makes income in an open world. The academics of economics have shown this theory to depend on certain critical assumptions. But it appeals to common sense.

In a broad sense, freer trade causes world wide incomes to equilibrate. Even now, China is starting to be regarded as a relatively high cost labour pool. All driven by export growth! What better way to cure the world's problems than to make poor people richer.

To add a little further cold water onto the protectionist fire, consider the form trade retaliation might take. Certainly raising tariffs on imported goods causes others to raise tariffs on your exports. But what if they become so retaliatory as to start placing tariffs on their exports – say oil from Canada, or Mexico, or copper from Chile etc. Ugly, self-defeating, and un-warranted, and a very real possibility.

In any case, there is no evidence to show globalization causes recessions.

Inflation Fighting

Faux Inflation

Was there ever any inflation to fight?

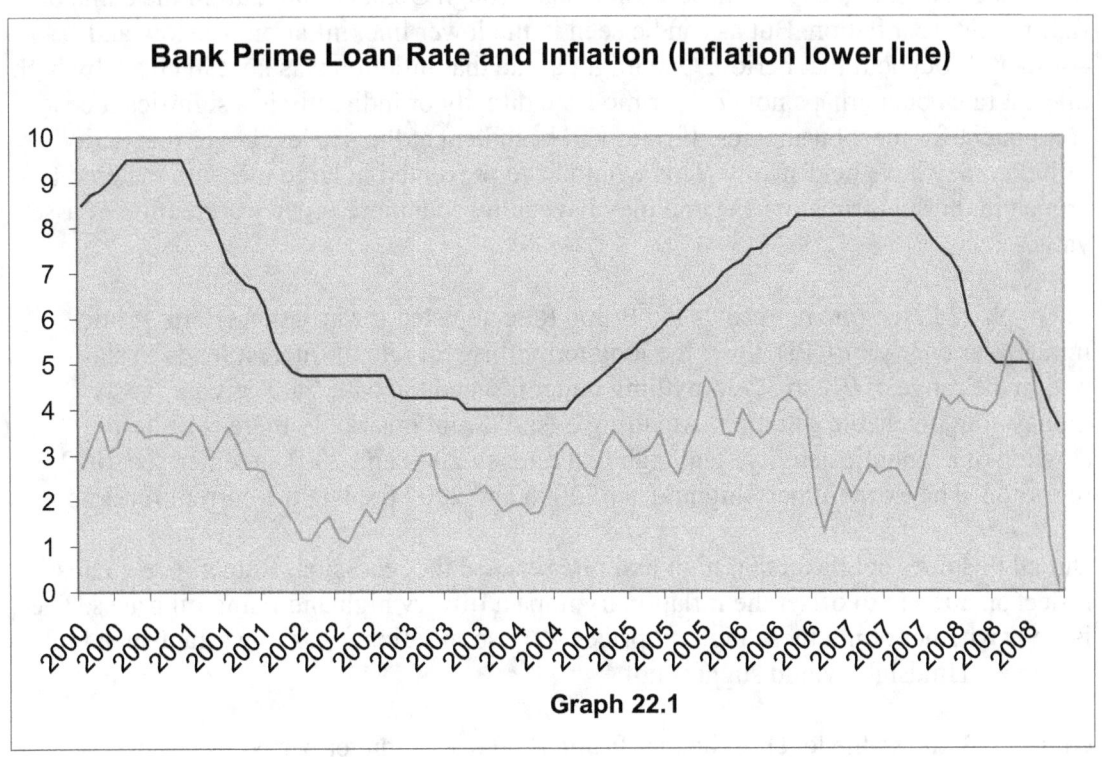

Bank Prime Loan Rate and Inflation (Inflation lower line)

Graph 22.1

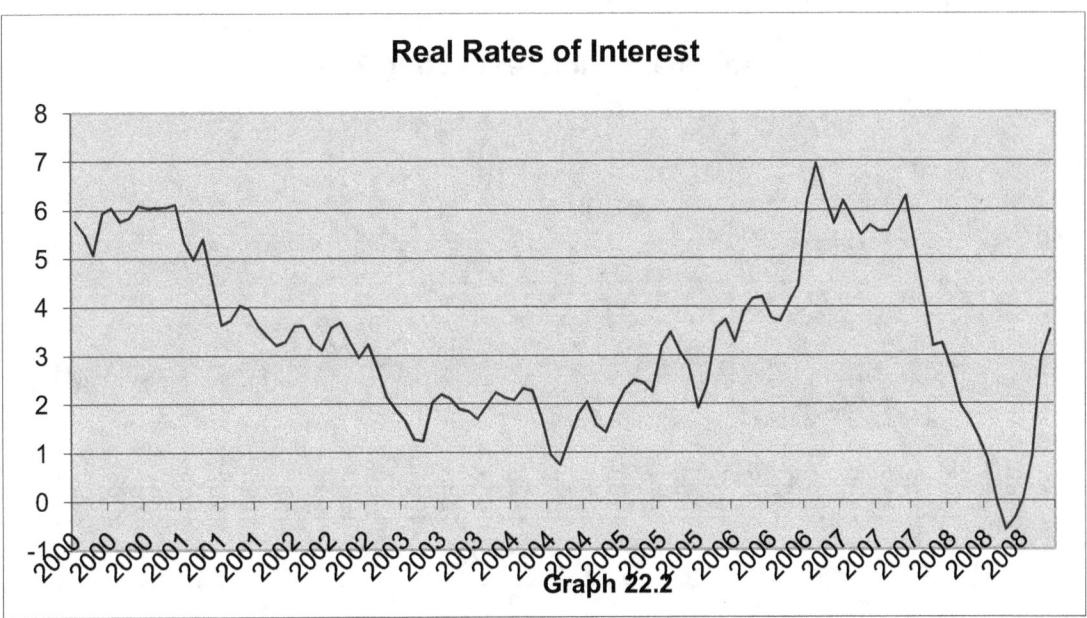

Real Rates of Interest

Graph 22.2

The *prime rate* is the interest rate commercial banks charge their most creditworthy customers - usually corporations. Inflation is represented by the year over year change in the CPI.

Graph 22.1 shows that the Prime rate was more than doubled from May 2004 to September 2006, and kept at these high levels through October 2007, all in the name of fighting future inflation. But as can be seen in the lower line, inflation was low and constant throughout that period. One might argue that inflation was kept in check by high interest rates but perhaps not. The Prime Rate directly or indirectly is a significant cost component for most businesses. If rates had been kept at the 4% level over this period, inflation may have held steady. This would have prevented in large measure the credit crunch in the sub-prime market and may have allowed a more orderly correction of asset values.

In Graph 22.2, the line represents the Prime Rate adjusted for inflation (Bank Prime minus year over year CPI). Over the long term, this real rate of interest tends to stay within the range of 0% to 3%. Anything under 0% and the banks are 'giving' away money – an untenable situation. Anything over 3% and invariably there is a sharp slowing of economic activity. The high real rates in 2000 and 2001 predated the 2002 recession. The extraordinary high rates of 2006 and 2007 predate the current recession.

But all this does not mean that high real rates caused the recession. Rather, these rates reflect an attempt to offset the inflationary impact of very high and rising oil prices. The issue is whether or not these high oil prices were so inflationary as to warrant such high real rates. Hindsight would suggest not.

Graph 23.1 shows the level of the real Prime Rate over a longer period.

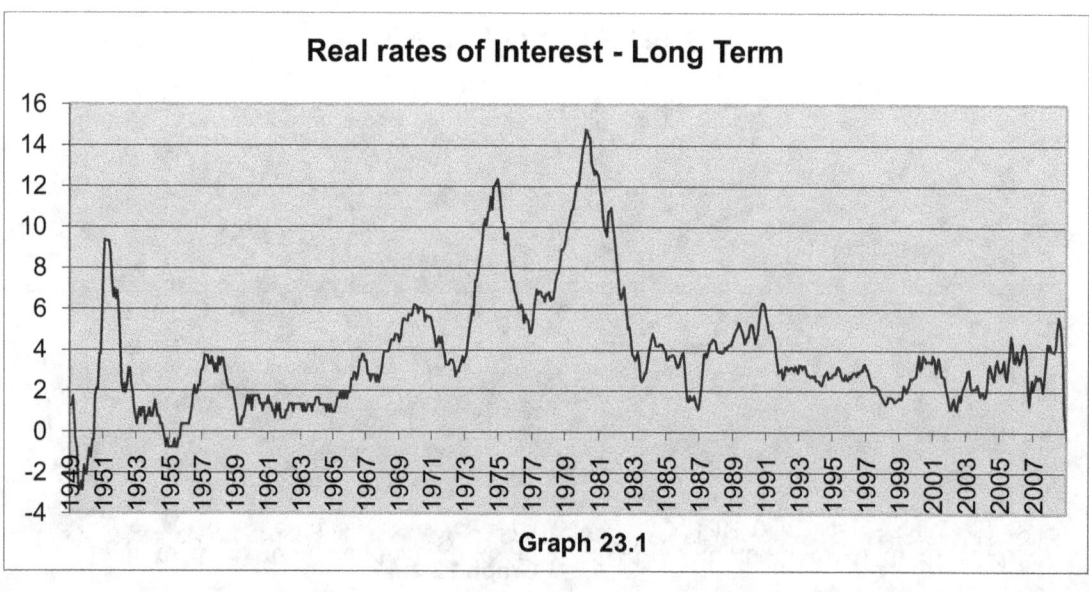

Graph 23.1

But let us consider the notion of inflation and ask whether it is a meaningful indicator. Should we be slaves to a distorted measure?

To begin with, it is impossible to obtain a measure of inflation which is statistically well-behaved. These theoretical issues have long been known. The early works of Afriat and of Deiwert showed clearly that none of the computed indexes (Paasche, Laspeyres, chained link relatives etc) meet all the 'well-behaved' criteria. The root of the problem lies in the fact that people constantly shift their consumption patterns, and/or are prone to buy completely new products which have no price history.

But in the modern age there is a much bigger problem. We have been undergoing a huge quality change in almost all of our consumer goods. Inflation indexes have no chance of taking this into account. Not only that, but consumers have been constantly shifting their consumption patterns; buying new goods and services and dropping old.

Consider a few examples:

Cameras: the shift from film to digital memory has led to faster developing, ability to take more pictures to get the 'right' one, easy and long-lasting storage of images. But the price of cameras has stayed fairly constant.

Computers: In the course of analyzing data for this book, I had need to sort 19,000 data points. As my experience with my old computers from the early nineties led me to expect some minutes of computation time to be required, I pushed back my chair to go get a coffee. But I had hardly let go of the mouse and the job was done. And of course we not only do the old jobs on the computer but a host of new ones – Net surfing, video encoding, long distance two-way communications (Skyping). All the while the price of a computer has remained fairly constant.

Think of the quality shifts in most consumer goods: household appliances, automobiles, airline flights, communications, wines, fruits and vegetables (greater variety and freshness due to transportation quality improvements), entertainment. In no way can an average price index take into account these quality changes and changing consumption patterns.

My common sense take on all this is that we are in the midst of a long term downward spiral of deflation. We are constantly getting more for less, and we are shifting our consumption from good to better, even while inflation indexes are rising.

There are two reasons why our misleading inflation indexes cause problems:

1. The authorities are constantly fighting a bogey that doesn't exist. The constrictionary monetary policy of recent years was unnecessary and has resulted in a collapse of business confidence which has turned a resolvable issue of high oil prices into a business rout.

2. Many business contracts are indexed i.e. they have inflation adjustment clauses. The most problematic of these are the indexed pensions in which future pension payments are 'topped up' to offset inflation. If, as I argue, there is no inflation in spite of the index values, then these pensioners are getting real pay raises at the cost of those not indexed.

The solution to this problem is for the government to stop producing official inflation numbers. Even changing the underlying computation of the CPI to include only the barest necessities (basket of food, rented shelter) would permit the continuation of indexed contracts but in a more just manner.

In summary, inflation data is overstated and misleading:

1. Quality improvements are everywhere.
2. New products are everywhere.
3. Inflation indexes are illogical.
4. Un-index COLA (Cost of Living Adjustment) contracts and pensions by redefining inflation. Concentrate on necessities.

The Great Recession of 09 was not caused by inflation, nor was it caused by the constrictionary policy of the Fed. It was accelerated and deepened by this policy.

In general, inflation is a straw horse; a windmill not to be attacked but to be avoided.

Other Causes

Greed

Did greed cause the Great Recession of 09? Surely not; greed has been with us a long time. All economics is predicated on greed. Perhaps it was excessive greed? But what does that mean? More greed than in the past? Successful, and blatant greed, may be the issue. Yet I think all of us continue to have faith in competition and open markets to keep greed at bay. The real issue is the closed market and anti-competitive forces at work.

The past, and surprisingly ongoing, high salaries, huge bonuses, and generous options, that are meted out to 'financial' executives and directors, are all taking place within the context of regulated companies. This is the other blade of the regulatory scissors; the economic rent blade. The economic rent, or un-earned economic surplus, arises because of the market protection afforded in the course of market regulation. The Left complain about greed but it is the Left's emphasis on regulation that allowed it to flourish.

As disgusting as they are, the extravagant pay packages in these regulated industries did not cause or even accelerate recessions.

There is a broader issue at stake with extravagant executive compensation. Berle and Means, writing over fifty years ago, noticed a trend towards the separation of ownership and control in publicly held corporations. They found that as corporations got larger, and the stock ownership of these corporations got dissipated, the management (control) were able to run these corporations with little regard to the stockholders (ownership). This is true today. Most of the large publicly traded corporation have their stock widely held. The largest shareholder in many modern corporations holds no more than a few percentages of the stock. Not only that, but many of the larger stock holders, e.g. pension funds, have no interest in corporate oversight duties; they simply buy and sell on the evidence of profits and dividends.

A corollary of the separation of ownership and control, usually overlooked, is that those in control of large corporations can decide for themselves what an appropriate pay level is for the executive. The surest and most non-controversial way for executives to be 'greedy' is to capture any growth of profits in bonuses and options while insulating their personal losses from corporate losses. In this manner, the large stock holders see steady dividends and profits (at least in good times) and the executives capture most if not all of the growth in profits.

The separation of ownership and control is not good for the economy. It distorts the distribution of resources in the economy and puts a brake on economic development. But again, this phenomenon has been with us many years and there is no evidence extant that shows correlation with recessions.

In summary then, extravagant executive pay levels can be attributed to two aspects of the modern economy:

1. Regulation, and
2. Separation of Ownership and Control.

What to do?

In the short run, tax the hell out of them. In the case of regulated corporations, put a progressive tax on incomes over $1m with the percentage ramping up to 99%. Pay lots of attention to what is included in income. Put together in a book all the resultant whining about how executive compensation needs to be very high to attract the best people, and make it a high school text. Hey, we all deserve a good laugh these days.

But wait! These are, for the most part, decent, law-abiding, very hard working people who have been handed the whole cookie jar. If their extravagant incomes were made illegally, the government can go after the monies so made. If their extravagant incomes were made through deceit then civil recourse can be had. But if these incomes were made legitimately, then who are we to be 'stealing' their income via our government. And what a Pandora's Box to open: nobody's income is safe under this type of regime.

In the long run, educate more, regulate less, and re-consider the role of Director of corporations.

None of this helps prevent recessions nor brings us out of the current one. But what better time to address these issues?

Lack of Regulation

Regulation of financial institutions, of one form or another, goes back to the time of Alexander Hamilton. Has the nature and form of regulation changed in recent years so as to be a cause of the Great Recession? Perhaps.

In 1987, control over 'near money' i.e. M2, was dropped. This coincided with the end of inflation-fighter Volcker's era, and the start of the academician's era under Greenspan. Mr Greenspan, under the Clinton regime, oversaw not only the easing of regulatory control, but also the 'encouragement' of home ownership through looser lending standards. Such policies may well have worked if the underlying asset values had held up. Further, as has been argued, these underlying asset values were not out of line with historical standards. So, on balance, monetary regulation has not caused the problem.

In a broader sense, financial regulation over the past 20 years has shifted towards monitoring illegal activity. Regulatory requirements, as a result, have shifted from control issues, to informational (reporting) issues. This is particularly true since the turn of the century. The shift to passive regulation was codified in the Sarbanes-Oxley Act of 2002.

Sarbanes-Oxley was implemented to counter the lax reporting standards that lead to the Enron 'scandal'. There is considerable controversy concerning the cost-benefit of the Act. Its reporting requirements are onerous, and its liability implications are daunting. Much of the cover-your-butt hokum at the end of most corporate news releases is a result of the Act. But it is passive in nature. It aims for transparency not control.

On balance then, the shift away from direct regulation of financial institutions to more passive information gathering may have had a part in the collapse of confidence in the sector, and the exacerbation of the downturn. But these regulatory trends have been taking place over many years and do not appear to be the immediate prime cause of the Great Recession.

Incompetence

Let us not brush this one aside too quickly.

We have all met people whose broad knowledge of world affairs borders on the comical. The state of scientific knowledge for a majority of the citizenry is low by First World Standards. Etc Etc Etc

Basically a bum rap. But suppose in degree it is true. Does this level of 'ignorance' cause a recession?

First, the phenomenon is not new, nor has it had a 'burst' recently.

Second, the underlying issue is perhaps one of specialization. We all hold in high esteem anybody who is 'good at their job'. And conversely. Self-esteem and the esteem of others turn on what you know that is useful not what is 'interesting'. We all experience the relish of competence shown by the 'lowest' workers in the industrialized world.

However, in the long run, broad knowledge, and general scientific knowledge, is necessary for dealing with ebbs and flows of future economic activity, and for keeping the ascendancy in geo-political matters.

But there is no cause of the Great Recession to be found here.

Unions

Over the past 25 years, the number of unionized workers has dropped from 17.7 million to 16.1 million. As a percentage of all employed wage and salary workers it has dropped from 20.1% to 12.4%. Not likely to be recession causing.

There are some issues of concern:

1. Unionism as a percentage of the workforce has risen from 12.1% in 2007 to 12.4% in 2008. This represents an increase of 428,000.
2. The Employee Free Choice Act almost passed in 2007: 241 to 185 in the House, cloture not invoked in the Senate. This Act would have mandated that unions could avoid a secret ballot and yet be recognized as representing the 'workers' if a majority of these workers had submitted vote cards in favour. The vote card system is non-private and subject to significant abuse. In one instance, in a vote card campaign documented by the National Labor Relations Board, a pro-union employee threatened a co-worker by saying that if she refused to sign the union card, "the union would come and get her children and that it would also slash her tires." There is not much doubt that this type of legislation will reappear in the next Congress given that so much labor money was poured into the Democratic campaign.

Both issues can negatively impact the international terms of trade (make America less competitive internationally). In turn, this can prolong the recession, and exaggerate the inevitable inflationary forces during the recovery.

Unionism, in general, requires us all to be vigilant against encroachment of our basic rights. Picket lines are fundamentally an exercise in illegal coercion. They have no other purpose than to bully or prevent replacement workers from reporting for work. Not only that, but there is constant pressure from unions to make picket line behaviour not subject to the standard laws of assault and battery. An example: in a recent labor dispute between one of Canada's largest companies and its union, management had to get a legal injunction to have the police enforce the basic laws regarding violence to persons. Management regarded this as a big success. In fact, it was disastrous. It is now on the books that union violence is OK unless there is a specific ruling from the judiciary in each instance. I once, in an earlier strike, had occasion to deal with a high ranking representative of the police in a matter of assault. A fellow replacement worker was assaulted as he was crossing the picket line. I indicated to the police that I could identify the culprit and that I had witnesses lined up. Instead of action I got a lot bafflegab which culminated in a statement to the effect: ..I didn't tell you this, but the police have made a practice to avoid getting involved in labor disputes ever since the General Strike of 1918....

And of course, the treatment of unions by the anti-trust folks is asymmetrical at best. The Big Three auto makers are not allowed to fix prices, but the unionized workers, with a common union, certainly can. This means that the UAW can capture the domestic economic rent of the industry resulting in prices very similar to those that would prevail if the domestic auto industry was a monopoly. The negative effect of this is evident for all to see these days.

The sad fact is that unionized wages are at the expense not of 'greedy' management but of non-unionized workers. To add insult to injury, the unions are now asking for bailouts, which again is at the expense of the non-unionized taxpayers.

I see nothing wrong with workers grouping together and marketing their services as one. Indeed management may well embrace this model as it solves many logistical issues in dealing with a workforce and keeping them productive and happy. But picket lines should be made illegal as they are prima facie vehicles for coercion. There must be no separate laws against violence or threats of violence as regards unionism. Anti-trust laws should be applied to union as well as to companies.

And above all: vigilance!

But as a cause of the Great Recession, we must press on.

Borrow to Buy

A number of commentators have suggested that the current malaise signals the end of the Borrow-to-Buy era. Warren Buffet, during a recent interview offered advice to young families to spend from savings.

I don't think so.

The Industrial Revolution of the eighteenth century was kick started, and made possible, by the Mercantilist trade boom founded on credit (essentially mortgage backed securities). The role of credit today is pervasive and essential for the smooth running of commerce.

Usury, and the use of credit, is what allows budding entrepreneurs to take a risk on their ideas. Credit is what allows businesses large and small to balance their inflows and outflows of cash in a rational manner. Credit is what allows consumers to elect to purchase now something which gives greater benefits now than if purchased in the future. And conversely, credit allows some consumers to save with interest and put off consumption until a more optimal time.

The use of credit is here to stay. Certainly the recent collapse in the value of assets has made some borrow-to-buy decisions look unwise. But at the time, and with the then current view of price trends, most of these decisions looked wise.

But has credit, or the abnormal growth in credit, caused the Great Recession?

No.

As can be seen in Graph 31.1, there is no indication that the size of credit (as measured by debt payments as a fraction of income) triggered any recession in the past 25 years. Also, there is no indication that the first derivative (the growth of this measure) is associated with recent recessions.

Perhaps most telling in Graph 30.1 is that the range in percentage of income paid out to service debt falls in a narrow range: 10% to 14.5%. Certainly no cause to panic.

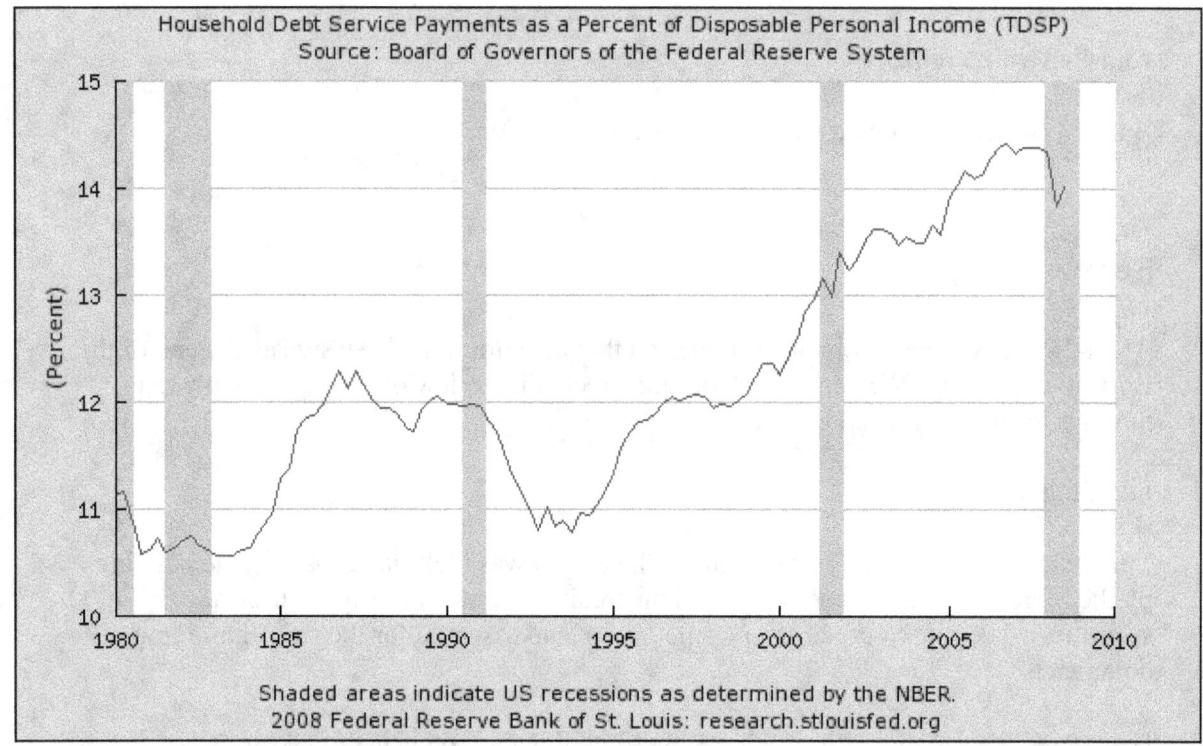

Graph 31.1

Summary – Cause

Many international commentators have suggested that America as an international force of commerce is finished. But if this is so, why did the US sub-prime crisis cause a worldwide Recession?

Two possible explanations:

1. The old dog hasn't died quite yet, or
2. A more world wide cause for the Great Recession can be found – oil.

Both are true. The first is obvious, and in any case is not considered in this book. The second has been considered in the above chapters.

Jumps in real oil prices have predated every recession since 1970. Subsequent falls in real oil prices have been associated with each recovery. No other cause has had such a connection. This is particularly true of the sub-prime crisis. Not only were the underlying assets not in a bubble, but the debt incurred to fund the purchase of these assets was not unduly large.

The main driver for the downturn was the huge jump in oil prices; the main driver for the ensuing panic was the draconian monetary policy which was focussed on an inflation that never existed and never arrived.

The Great Depression vs. the Great Recession

There are three names associated with the Great Depression: Hoover, Roosevelt, and Keynes. President (1929-1933) Herbert Hoover caused the Depression, President (1933-1945) Franklin Roosevelt cured the Depression, and John Maynard Keynes, economist, supplied the theoretical tools for the cure. None of it true, but that is the general perception to this day.

Let's start with Keynes. His magnum opus, The General Theory of Employment, Interest and Money, was not written until 1936 so the New Deal was not born of Keynesian theories. Keynes refers to Roosevelt and the New Deal on p. 331 of the book; difficult to do if his book brought about those policies!

The traditional interpretation of Keynes work was that he advocated deficit funding of fiscal stimulus to offset collapse of consumer demand in a recession. The General Theory however, mentions government deficits only twice, p. 98, and pp. 128-30. At no point does he appear to be advocating deliberate use of deficits to stimulate the economy. His theory held that taxing a dollar from the consumer and using it for government expenditure had a stimulus effect (in a Recession) because it spent that part of the consumer's dollar that would have been saved. In other words, Keynes was a tax and spend stimulator, not a deficit stimulator. Nor did he advise such policies from a liberal point of view: he advised the use of fiscal policy for stimulus purposes not for activist government policy on infrastructure and other societal purposes.

Keynes view of monetary policy was that in times of recession its effectiveness was blunted by the 'Liquidity trap': monetary stimulus simply led to more hoarding of cash. This view has never really been tested. Enough money, and enough debasing of the currency, will soon put a stop to hoarding as a way of protecting value.

Keynes's General Theory is unlike modern economics treatises with their advanced mathematics and mind numbing graphs. Keynes had only one diagram in the entire book. He had only three data tables that show exactly thirty two numbers. Nowhere to be found are the traditional Keynesian graphs of IS LM functions. Such precise graphical interpretations of what Keynes really said were left to post-War economists such as John Hicks. Many PhD theses have been written interpreting what Keynes's really meant to say. What he really did say is unclear to this day so it can hardly have had that big an influence during the Depression.

This gives us a caution: a cure for the current Great Recession is not to be found in the Great Depression 'cure' of deficit fiscal stimulus. Keynes should be taken lightly.

Let's consider President Hoover (President 1929 – 1933). There are a lot of parallels between his presidency and that of President George W Bush. Both were unfairly tagged with causing the downturn. Both were given no credit for trying to implement cures for the symptoms if not the cause of the downturn. Both were shabbily treated by 'friend' and foe alike. And both will be treated with much more kindness and respect by history.

It is now generally understood that all the New Deal programs found their genesis in the Hoover administration. Hoover was a technological activist, a Technocrat type, one who believed the future lay in the application of technology to solve commercial problems. He practised what he preached. He was a very respected mining engineer, having created a flotation system for the Broken Hill mine in Australia (in use to this day), and having written a definitive textbook on mining engineering. With this background, he was appointed Secretary of Commerce in 1920, a post he held until his election to the presidency.

Hoover's activist approach resulted in the implementation of policies which in some cases depended on voluntarism, but in other cases made use of fiscal 'stimulus'. He was consistently a Keynesian, both as Commerce Secretary and as President. However he was not a deficit stimulator: his tax increases in 1932 to pay for his 'New Deal' programs, exacerbated the Depression, and his inability to rein in the Smoot-Hawley anti-trade Act also contributed. At the time, he was generally credited with having caused the Depression (although only in power for eight months) and with having no solution for it. He was generally reviled domestically and internationally. It did not help that FDR took a petty dislike to Hoover.

History has been kind to Hoover: he is credited with having laid the groundwork for the Marshall Plan after WWII, and his dam has been re-renamed from Boulder to Hoover.

"Twenty million people are starving. Whatever their politics, they shall be fed!"...
Hoover

Franklin Delano Roosevelt (President 1933-1945) was popular from the beginning. His New Deal policies and his 'Keynesian' fiscal regime are generally credited with alleviating and ultimately curing the Depression. No matter that all this false; he remains posthumously as popular as ever.

Roosevelt focussed on the poor in society. His liberal programs were popular and took the edge off the extreme hardship, but they did not alleviate unemployment and they did not cure the Depression. Indeed, his pro-Union and anti-business policies contributed to a worsening of the Depression with the recession of 1937-38. Only when his policies were reversed did this latter recession recede. Roosevelt was only Keynesian in the classical sense: tax and spend. He did not run up a significant deficit until after 1938, the effect of which was too late to effect a cure for either the Depression, or the additional recession of the late thirties.

So both Hoover and Roosevelt were Keynesian in their tax and spend policies but both were not ultra Keynesians in the sense of spend but don't tax (deficit spending). Looking to Roosevelt 'stimuli' to justify today's monster fiscal deficits as a Depression/Recession cure would be wrong.

But what did cause the Depression?

The traditional and widely accepted view is that unduly lax monetary policy allowed a huge and unwarranted run-up in asset prices, creating a bubble which burst in Oct of 1929 and drove a stake into the heart of business confidence. The ensuing period of deflation was countered with neither monetary policy nor fiscal policy. Roosevelt, with his New Deal, liberal, policies cured the Depression.

Wrong!

To be sure money was easy in the late twenties: most anyone could buy stocks on margin, with as little as 10% down. But margin requirements are generally not the purview of government policy but rather of the stock markets and the individual lenders. They must surely have believed that the underlying asset values would not collapse thus endangering their loans. Why would they believe that? There was a lot of optimism is the twenties about the very technological impacts on business that Hoover was focussed on. Furthermore the methods of mass production introduced by Henry Ford were starting to spread through all major industries with salutary effects. But were assets bid up to stratospheric height by these trends? No. At no time during this period were real estate prices bubbly. What about stock prices? The best data I can find indicates that that the PE ratios of the senior traded stocks were around 20 at the peak. Compare this to the historical average of 15, and the peak in 2008 of 30. Here is the thing: there is no proper, or best, or appropriate PE ratio; it simply reflects the current view of stock investors about the future prospects of the underlying businesses. Given the productivity improvements of the twenties, a PE of 20 was not 'extravagant'. So there was no bubble of assets to trigger the panic.

But what did trigger the panic?

Restrictive monetary policy.

Same today!

If the authorities had pushed more cash into the system the prices would have been supported and at the very least the pullback could have been manageable. Same today.

The authorities in 1929 were fighting an inflation that didn't exist. Look at the CPI in Graph 37.1 – no inflation there.

Graphs can be quite instructive.

In graph 36.1, below, the annual federal surplus/deficit is shown. Clearly there was no ultra Keynesian stimulus until the early war years (WWII).

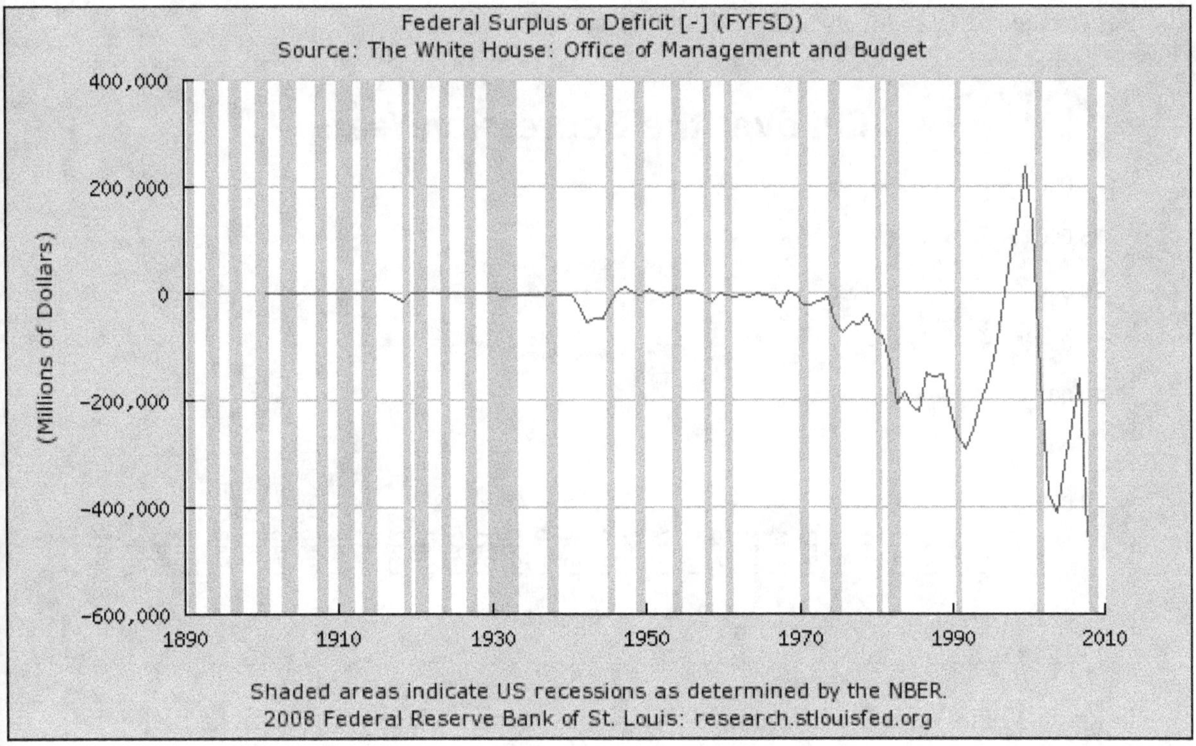

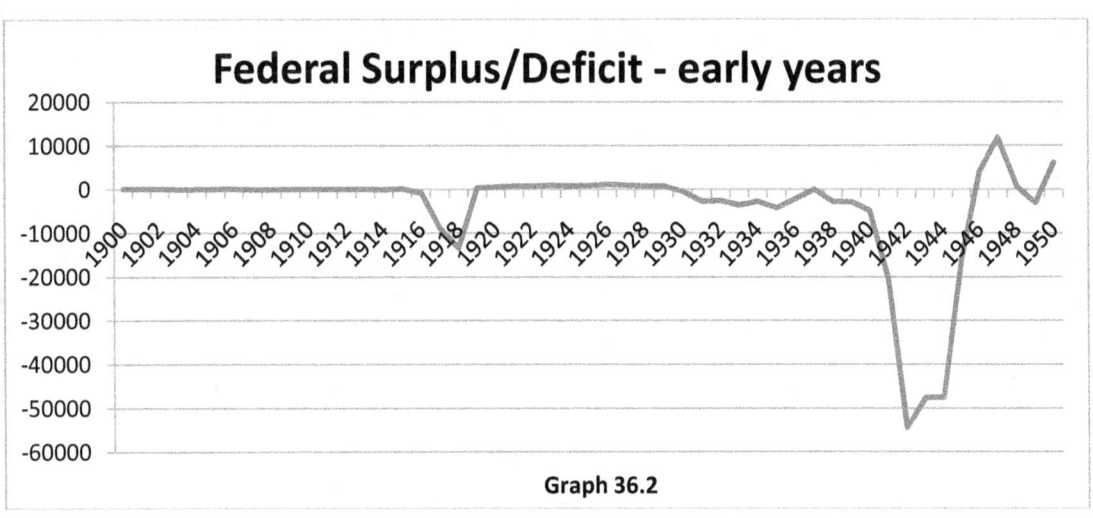

Federal Surplus or Deficit [-] (FYFSD)
Source: The White House: Office of Management and Budget
400,000
200,000
0
-200,000
-400,000
-600,000
(Millions of Dollars)
1890
1910
1930
1950
1970
1990
2010
Shaded areas indicate US recessions as determined by the NBER.
2008 Federal Reserve Bank of St. Louis: research.stlouisfed.org

Graph 36.1

In this next one, graph 36.2, we see that in spite of the 'massive' tax increase of 1932, Hoover actually kicked off a deficit era carried on by Roosevelt. However, this deficit is so small that it is more likely a case of intended taxes not catching up with intended spending because of the slowdown. Not really an ultra Keynesian effort.

Federal Surplus/Deficit - early years
20000
10000
0
-10000
-20000
-30000
-40000
-50000
-60000
1900
1902
1904
1906
1908
1910
1912
1914
1916
1918
1920
1922
1924
1926
1928
1930
1932
1934
1936
1938
1940
1942
1944
1946
1948
1950

Graph 36.2

In graph 37.1, the CPI (Consumer Price Index) is plotted over the Depression. Prices never reached 1929 levels until well into World War II.

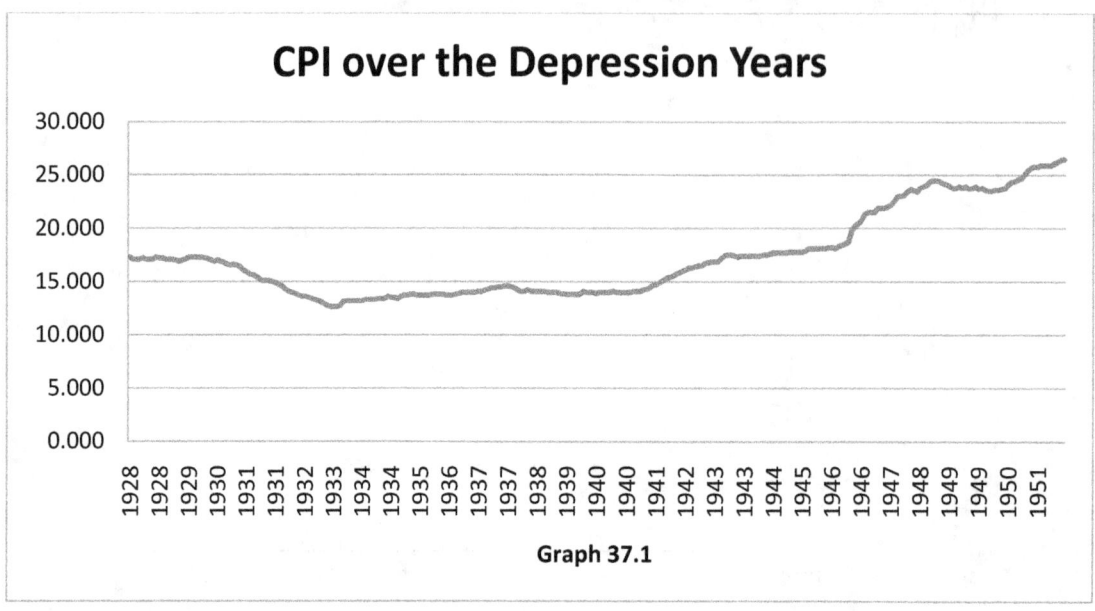

In graph 37.2, we see the CPI plotted over a longer span. Clearly, deflation had set in by 1925, and prices were basically flat in the previous five years. Prices, at their peak in 1929 were below that of most of the twenties and well below the peak in 1920.

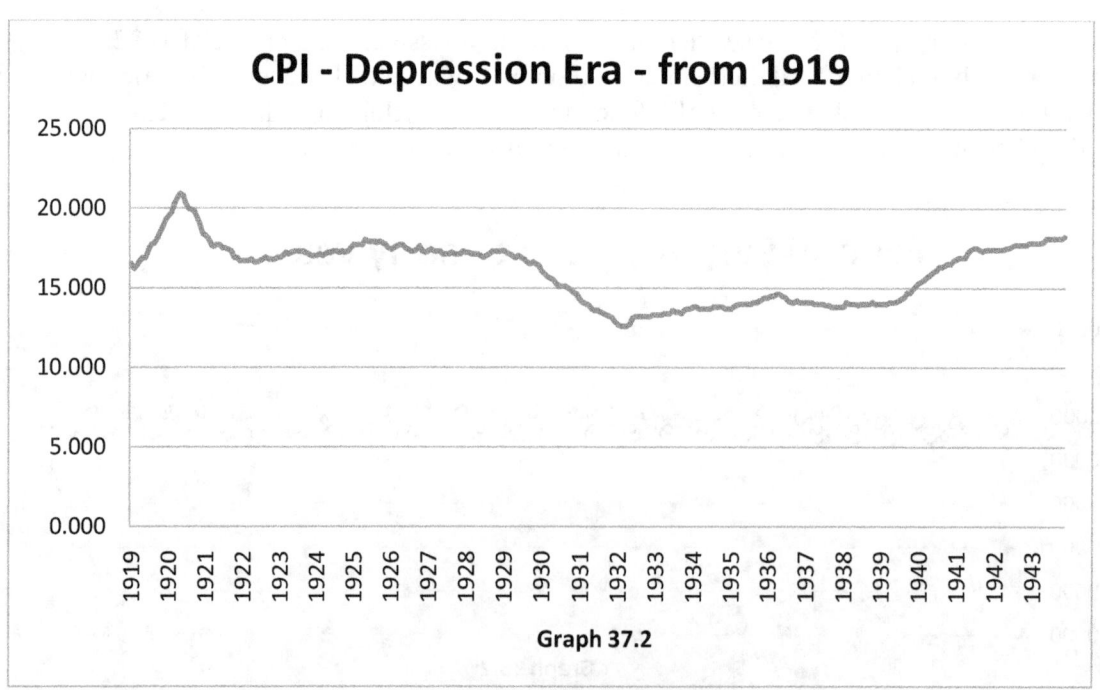

One last look at the Federal deficit. Graph 38.1 shows it over a longer period. The Hoover stimulus of 1931 and 1932 was little increased by Roosevelt. The small stimulus deficit of 1938 had hardly any impact on the 1937 recession and more likely reflects ramping up to wartime expenditures.

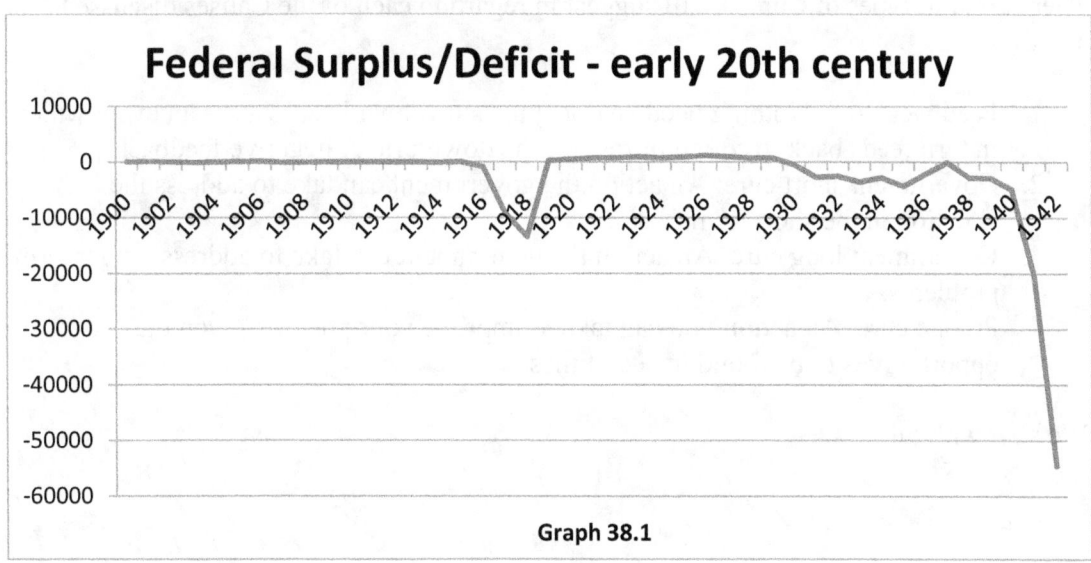

So all considered, it looks to me like the Depression was triggered by a panic caused not by bloated asset prices but by an overly restrictive monetary policy incapable of funding the productivity driven growth which was underway by 1929. The Depression was sustained by a continuation of restrictive monetary policy even in the face clear deflation. The shrinkage of international trade, in part triggered by the Smoot-Hawley Act, added to the constriction. But the real problem was the structural shifting of production from that which was working (cars, housing, food) to New Deal stop gap measures. Roosevelt didn't end the Depression; he extended it.

The parallel to the situation in early 2009 is downright spooky.

The Cures

There are four types of Cures I will suggest in regard to each of the Causes discussed. They are:

1. Feedback cure: Nothing need be done; the slowdown itself causes an event which in turn feeds back to soften or reverse the downturn. A negative feedback.
2. Government short cure: An action the government can take to address the situation in the short term.
3. Government long cure: An action the government can take to address longer term problems.
4. Private cure: An action you can take to improve your position given the opportunities to be found in such times.

We start with oil.

Low Oil Prices

First and foremost, neither the U.S. government nor the individual can control oil prices. Both however can buy, or sell, oil if that contributes to a cure.

Feedback cure: Oil prices have plummeted during the slowdown. This removes the main cause of the downturn. A classic negative feedback situation. Low oil prices pull the rug out from inflationary pressure and make possible an expansionary monetary policy.

Government short cure: Buy oil with government monies – anyway possible – thus causing an infusion of purchasing power into the economy. Fight deflation now; fight inflation later.

Government long cure: Buy, and sell oil, using government monies – anyway possible. The threshold price is the big issue here: my reading of the charts suggests a conservative policy would be to buy oil below $60 and sell it above. Why? Very low oil prices cannot hold – any kind of a recovery and they will pop – alternate energy use will not really get into full swing until the oil price is higher and/or time passes so the industrial structure can adjust. Why sell over $60?: to make a bit of money for the government, to prevent a brake on the recovery, and to reflect that alternative energy use eventually will keep oil price low.

Private cure: Buy oil stocks with large, secure, and relatively cheap reserves. I particularly like the oil companies that have a stake in the deep monster fields in the Gulf of Mexico. Timing is everything however.

Discussion: The all important issue is that given a recovery, and given the growth of the third world both in population, and in incomes, the demand for oil is going to pop, and alternatives cannot be brought on stream fast enough.

My bet is on electric cars. An all electric car is very much simpler to make, ultimately, than either an internal combustion car, or a hybrid. Just bits of stuff and very few moving parts. I predict all electric, safe, sedans, for under $10,000. An electric company executive recently told me that roughly twenty percent of vehicles could be electric before there is a significant push on electricity capacity or prices. This is mainly because of car charging being done in low demand times (night), and because of advances in grid management.

What about the criticism that electricity generation is 'dirty'. Need not be! If the government put a cost on the pollution, and on the unsafe disposal, practices of the electric companies, they would generate perfectly clean electricity. This certainly applies to coal; there are many known, more costly, ways of generating clean electricity from coal. It is just that the coal generators have not had government 'encouragement' to go the clean route. Likewise for nuclear. Pebble bed reactors, and potentially, traveling-wave generators, are a bit more expensive but are as safe as any generating system. Furthermore, the waste can be recycled, and ultimately destroyed by plasma – if the cost incentive is there.

So let me add to the government long cure: set up price wedges to ensure that private industry generates a clean product (and lots of it). In the end, I think clean safe nuclear power will be needed to meet the ultimate demand.

Of course any efforts on dragging the economy off oil dependence have the added salutary effect of making nations less dependant on others for such critical inputs. Geopolitically speaking, nuclear is a necessity.

High Asset Prices

Lenders Lending

The current ill-feeling towards bank bailouts may be unfair and unwarranted. The senior banks were 'nudged' by the monetary authorities into taking up the Fanny Mae and Freddie Mac securities. Certainly, if oil prices had not burst upward, and if the monetary authorities had been fighting deflation instead of inflation, the banks would have remained sound. So:

Feedback cure: Sorry, no self-correcting mechanism here. Collapsing values of subprime mortgages and other assets leads to further price collapse.

Government short cure: Buy these toxic assets. Only fair: the Democratic administration of Clinton created the mess, the Democratish Congress during the Bush years failed to address the mess, so the Democratic regime of President Obama should help those affected. This policy has the added effect of pushing cash into the economy (via the banks) and thereby contributing to the liquidity cure. Additionally, buy any other senior paper available until this Recession has turned.

Government long cure: Don't throw the baby out with the bathwater. The idea of increasing the equity position of households seems worthy. Fanny Mae and Freddie Mac should be regulated less not more, but rules for greater transparency should be introduced.

Private cure: Taking out a sub-prime mortgage, if possible, may be wise. House prices are low, and interest rates can be locked in at around 5%. If you can keep up the payments, now may be a good time. Of course, many other assets are worthy of consideration.

The FOMC should be buying not only toxic assets but also other senior assets held by the banks. This will cause the banks to be cash rich and asset poor and will have no option but to start lending again.

Rising Real Estate Prices

The key here is the wealth effect: rising asset values make consumers feel better off and more amenable to consumption spending – a good thing during a Recession. Falling asset values make them feel poor and they restrict consumption – a bad thing.

Feedback cure: nothing automatic here.

Government short cure: Keep interest rates low and money flowing into the economy (create money if need be). In effect debase the currency and thereby make other assets more valuable. Also tax incentives for first time buyers and buyers of foreclosed properties, and other incentives for home ownership instead of renting, are all appropriate in these times.

Government long cure: Transparency is key. If mortgage lenders know the underlying risk/reward factors they will be more inclined to lend and to lend rationally. Government may well have a role in disseminating information on changes in demographics, household incomes, and growth/decline forces at work in specific geographic areas.

Private cure: Difficult to tell at the moment whether stock equity, or real estate equity, is the better way to go. Buy both and be safe. Timing is everything though. Low interest rates should be encouraging such buying. Consider: at 10% borrowing costs, you need the asset to double in 7 years to offset these costs – at 5% you need the asset to double over 12 years –surely the Great Recession will not last that long!

A Ten Thousand Dow

Again, the consumption impact of high and rising asset prices is important here. Considering that productivity in the American economy is high and rising, that input costs, including energy, are falling, and that technological advances continue apace, then the Dow by any standards is well below trend.

Feedback cure: There is some negative feedback here: low stock prices encourage investors to switch out of other assets (cash, bonds, etc) and into equities. This in turn puts upward pressure on prices.

Government short cure: Get more cash into the hands of the banks, other institutions and tax payers – as fast as possible. But go further: have all government departments invest in equities – most importantly the FOMC which in effect can create money to buy equities. Stick to the blue chips. Sell as the economy recovers. DO NOT interfere in the running of these companies.

Government long cure: Back out of these equity positions: Holding illiquid investments is not the role of government once the pump is primed and the stock market is recovering.

Private cure: As before, and bears repeating: Difficult to tell at the moment whether stock equity, or real estate equity, is the better way to go. Buy both and be safe. Timing is everything though. Low interest rates should encourage us all to be buying. Consider: at 10% borrowing costs, you need the asset to double in 7 years to offset these costs – at 5% you need the asset to double over 12 years –surely the Great Recession will not last that long!

A healthy Dow is very important for the cure: The wealth effect has a big impact on consumption spending.

Deficits

Reduction of the Domestic Deficit / Debt

If you believe in the ultra Keynesian cure, you should increase the deficit not the opposite. If you are Galbraithian in your beliefs, you should incur deficits to build up infrastructure.

There is an argument for deficits at any time: if the government can borrow money and get a greater return on it than the cost, it is justified. If it costs a $1B to build a freeway, and that freeway contributes net more than $1B (discounted present value) to the economy then surely borrowing for it is justified. Similarly if a deficit, run to fund healthcare, returns more than its cost in greater productivity of the economy then it is justified. But is it? The problem lies in the distribution of benefits and costs. In all such cases, government will be incurring debt on behalf of some taxpayers who will not see sufficient benefits to warrant the future costs. It is the classic problem with any government spending. Some pay and do not receive much benefit; others pay and receive a disproportionate benefit. There is no solution to this problem. We all sin on this one. Even the most diehard Republican wants government to spend money on law-and-order, and on the military. But same issue. Some who are taxed, or who run up a deficit, do so under duress. A pure Libertarian would say all government tax/debt is theft: let the free market build the roads and charge tolls etc. Won't work!

But whatever we believe about deficits, surely they have a stronger justification in a recession with its coincident deflation. Stuff can be bought cheaper now than later.

So:

Feedback cure: In an ultra Keynesian sense there is some negative feedback – government expenditures stay the same but tax revenues decrease because of the slowdown thus causing an automatic deficit and in turn, if you believe it, cause a stimulation to the economy.

Government short cure: If a deficit does put more cash in the hands of consumers then it is a part of the cure. A deficit to buy oil, or buy some toxic and other assets is good.

Government long cure: Deficits are bad! Why? Because like any chronic borrower it removes the spur for responsible fiscal behaviour. Best to avoid deficit spending for anything but critical infrastructure/ social objectives except in times of deflation when a more liberal approach is needed.

Private cure: Just like the government, a little bit of deficit in a time of deflation can be fiscally wise.

Reduction of the External Deficit / Debt

In and of themselves the external deficit and debt do not cause nor cure recessions. But here you can't print money and 'escape' the consequences. The piper must be paid. Oil is the main culprit. If America were free of a foreign dependency on oil, and better, if America had abundant and inexpensive domestic energy, the terms of trade would alter radically in her favour. Low cost labor elsewhere would be more than offset by technological advancements in materials and processes. Furthermore low cost labor becomes high cost labor; that is the whole genius behind open markets.

But as regards the Great Recession nothing more need be said.

Open Markets

Made in America

Apart from fluffy words, any government encouragement of Made in America is anti-open markets and invites retaliation sooner or later. Furthermore, in a time of Recession it makes the situation worse. The widely accepted view of the impact of the Smoot-Hawley Act on the Depression is instructive. So:

Feedback cure: Bad. A positive feedback – a downturn triggers protectionist policies which in turn contribute to the downturn.

Government short cure: Give in as little as possible. Focus on expansionary monetary policy instead of expansionary fiscal policy and you sidestep the issue.

Government long cure: Create a full free trade arrangement with Canada (locks down access to a treasure of natural resources if nothing else!). Create a full free trade arrangement with Australia –same reasons. And these are your friends. Create free trade with your enemies. If you think your political regime is superior to theirs, open markets are the best demonstration of these benefits (they see your results first hand).

Private cure: Sure, go ahead, Buy America – products made in America are generally of very high quality.

Deflation Fighting

Now we come to the crux of it all.

To start with, let us acknowledge that there is a built in bias amongst the key players towards fighting inflation. Most, if not all, of the decision makers are successful, careful people who have much of their hard earned money in interest bearing instruments. They are loathe to see the purchasing power of these assets deteriorate via inflation. On the other hand, a little deflation makes the value of their husbanded monies increase.

The situation of the struggling household is quite different. A little inflation is nothing to worry about, but deflation means insecurity in the workplace. Indeed, to most people, moderately rising prices presents opportunities for entrepreneurship. Would you start a business in which prices are falling?

I suggest that the decision makers have a bias different from the vast majority of those affected by their decisions.

Worse.

The statistics on which the decision makers act are flawed or illogical. The CPI and the PPI are aggregates that theoreticians have long counselled against accepting as untainted. Notwithstanding the use of such 'fancy' concoctions as Laspeyeres Index, Paasche Index, or Chained Link Relatives, they all have drawbacks which render them incapable of giving a 'correct' read on what is intended. It is a matter of mixing apples and oranges.

Worse still.

The changes in consumption patterns over time, and the massive changes in the quality of the standard products, can in no way be properly measured in an 'index'. The bias is clearly towards over reporting inflation.

What to do?:

Feedback cure: Deflation, the twin of Recession, is supposed to stimulate demand i.e. a negative feedback. Quite obviously, consumers are thinking a step ahead: lower prices engender an expectation of even lower prices. Result: the slowdown is accelerated and the expectation self-fulfils. So no help here.

Government short cure: Take a severe downturn as prima facie evidence that deflation is the problem. Infuse the economy with cash by using the FOMC to purchase not just government debt instruments, but corporate senior debt, corporate senior equities, and oil. The FOMC, the Federal Open Market Committee, reports to the Federal Reserve Board of Governors, and Mr Bernanke. The Committee is charged with sopping up liquidity or infusing liquidity, by buying and selling securities held by the Federal Reserve Banks, and other institutions. The Committee operates through the Federal Reserve Bank of New York. In exchange for purchasing securities, it creates a debit account for the purchase amount at the Federal Reserve Bank. If ultimately this puts a call on cash, the FOMC can approve the printing of currency. In this way, the FOMC can increase the money supply. Conversely, the FOMC can 'cancel' money by selling securities to the Reserve Banks.

Government long cure: Stop producing inflation statistics. Alternatively, only produce a 'necessities of life' index and call that the CPI. That way, indexed contracts will be set to grow only if the price of the necessities grow. Allow some inflation (say 5%) to offset quality improvements as a result of technological change. Reconsider the theory that when a fundamental input, such as oil, jumps in price, that cost inflation should be muted by restrictive monetary and fiscal policy. Perhaps a better policy is to let the cost increase of the input be reflected in overall inflation increases so that everyone is nudged away from consumption towards savings.

My reading of the statistical evidence is that fighting inflation was the key policy error in both the Great Depression, and the Great Recession of 09.

Let us consider some of the key actors in this drama. The Treasury Secretary under the George W Bush administration often acted like a deer in the headlights. When the downturn got underway in late 2008, he asked Congress for almost $1T to bail out the banks by buying toxic assets. But within a few weeks he was using the bulk of the money for other purposes. Furthermore, in the face of clear evidence that he and his Dept had not made any accurate forecasts of late, he made speeches announcing how bad the downturn would be. In his role, such statements have the nature of self-fulfilling prophecies. Avoiding making public forecasts might be best.

Over at the Fed, Mr too-little-too-late Bernanke kept announcing that he would, in the near future, lower interest rates, without actually doing so. Perhaps he held to the view, common among economists, that announcing a policy removes the need for actually implementing it: the economy will act in advance of policy as if the policy had been implemented etc etc. In retrospect, the opposite happened: it gave the message that the economy was getting worse without the assurance of a compensating lowering of interest rates. Mr Bernanke has been prone to making dismal forecasts (my wife refers to him as Cranky Bernanke). I suggest he replace the nameplate on his desk with a two sided sign: Silence is Golden. Recently (early March 09) he did allow that the recovery could start by the end of the year, and surprise, the market went up. But better for the market to ignore such rash forecasts, and better for Mr Bernanke to hush up.

The current Treasury Secretary comes from the bowels of the system that generated this mess. Perhaps he is best to address the problems. But what other industry would put the very people who create the mess in charge of cleaning it up. Even the auto industry would tend to fire people who evidenced such incompetence, and most definitely when they are paid huge dollars because they are so 'expert'.

Just how do you fire a member of the Federal Reserve Board?

The Obama administration appears to be combating the Recession with fiscal stimulus. But are they? The budget brought down in February 2009 sets aside massive funds for Health, Infrastructure, Energy alternatives, and Education. But in presenting his budget, President Obama made it clear that he intends to cut other programs and 'fat' such that the deficit will actually decrease. So what we have here is neither ultra Keynesian stimulus, nor Keynesian stimulus. Essentially the budget is a liberal agenda with an eye to fiscal conservatism. I would argue this is a good budget. It doesn't pretend to stimulate the economy out of recession – hopefully he will nudge monetary policy into a more aggressive mode. And surely, even to those with a free market focus, the productive benefits of a healthier population, fewer potholes in the roads, independence from foreign oil, and a smarter workforce, is obvious. Government doesn't actually have to do the work, just fund it. Open bidding would be good.

We cannot do much about oil except buy some, but we can focus on the real solution to the Great Recession by combating deflation with aggressive monetary policy. Debase the currency: make hoarding less attractive, and bump up consumption spending through the wealth effect via increased values in stocks and real estate.

To those who worry about the international effects of debasing the currency, let me put it this way:

Beware the Sarkozy!

Elegance and eloquence can mask the fact that his self-interest does not align with that of America.

As to the World Bank, and the IMF, I wouldn't take them too seriously. They stood by while Argentina stole the assets of the Bank of Nova Scotia. They stood buy while Ecuador stole the assets of Encana. They are standing by while Ecuador reneges on its international debt obligations even while it collects massive oil revenues. They stood by while Venezuela stole the assets of Occidental and other oil companies, and they are standing by while Venezuela is stealing the assets of Agrium. To be sure these institutions are 'concerned', and have it all under study, and are using diplomatic channels as much as they can. But they are ineffectual.

A made in America, for Americans, monetary policy is needed to combat the Great Recession, to the benefit of all of us.

Other Cures

Policy on Religion versus Greed

Are people really greedy? What is meant by that term?

Certainly people act in their self interest, sometimes in a very narrow sense.

But does this behaviour cause a recession, or prevent recovery?

No! Not one way or the other.

The economy could adapt to an aggressively acquisitive society, or to an ascetic, contemplative, back-to-the-earth one. In the one case the GDP would be high, in the other low, but neither need lead to a Recession nor prevent a recovery. The nature of a recession lies not in the level of economic activity, but rather in the unintended consequences inherent in the process. People are not unemployed because they chose to be.

Of course there is the issue of the generous compensation systems set up by the cabal of executives that run the financial system. In good times, dealing in billions of dollars, nobody seems to notice the few million here or there that is skimmed off by the intermediaries (the financial executives). But perhaps it is time to focus on issues such as: is there sufficient competition in the industry? Is regulation giving a monopolistic cover to the industry? And are the principals too readily able to apportion profits to themselves?

In the midst of a Recession, focussing on the 'greed' of the key players deflects from the solution of the problem. Furthermore, in the grand scheme of things, the numbers are not large enough to have an impact on the overall economy. We should be indignant, but we should keep our eye on the ball. Deflation is the problem! Consider this: these overpaid executives either made their money legally or they did not. If done legally, it would be a dangerous precedent to take it away from them. If done illegally, there are other remedies, and they should be applied.

So:

Feedback cure: NA

Government short cure: NA

Government long cure: If an industry is regulated, make sure that the monopolistic nature of the industry does not cause 'inappropriate' aggrandizing of profits to the principals. If the industry is not regulated, back off. Progressive taxation (higher percentage tax on higher incomes) has traditionally been used to address these 'extravagant' incomes, but that is a two edged sword. Any interference with the market price mechanism has a distorting effect on the economy. A thought: tax consumption not income – if the very rich want to plough back their riches via investment, why not – who better to make such investments than those with a proven track record. Their consumption, on the other hand, uses up resources for personal use.

Private cure: no comment.

Increase Regulation

Educate don't regulate.

Make business dealings transparent; enact laws to effect this.

In any case, that horse is in the next county. No sense in closing the door now.

Increased regulation will likely accelerate the downturn and certainly will not counter it.

More money for Universities

Not relevant to the matters at hand. Certainly the very best economists, from the very best universities, working in the very best financial firms, let us get into this mess. Perhaps the University of common sense is where the money should be flowing.

Anti-trust Laws applied to Unions

Only fair!

Would definitely increase productivity in the long run.

Would enhance America's position in the world.

Not relevant to the matters at hand.

Save-to-Buy

In the early stages of this downturn, Oprah Winfrey had a show focussed on how the consumer can consume less. Wise in the small. But gosh. That advice leads to the following causal chain: Downturn leads to frugality leads to further downturn leads to further frugality leads to …

Even Mr Buffet, a few months ago, about the time he was publicly announcing that he was buying GE on the open market (at $21 – it is now $6), stated in an interview that young people should buy only from savings. Now that is rich folks talk. How do budding entrepreneurs get started but for borrowing. How do young folks get a car to get to work except through borrowing? How do renters break into the housing market except for borrowing? Mr Buffet's advice would wind us back to the pre-Mercantilist era. Economic history suggests that the flowering of commerce in the mercantilist era was due to the use of letters of credit. In turn the robust Mercantilist era was a necessary pre-condition for the industrial revolution. What's next?: barter so that debasing of currency is impossible?

There have been a number of so called experts announcing in the media that this Recession marks the end of the borrow-to-buy era. Absolute nonsense!

Certainly in a downturn that is the worst possible advice.

All of the Above Cures

No!

Some of the Above Cures

Yes!

Let us now consider, briefly, some other cures suggested for dealing with the Recession:

Extend the sector-specific and company-specific bailout program

This favors the unsuccessful over the successful.

This rewards the high cost industry/company over the low cost industry/company.

This results in lower paid workers subsidizing higher paid workers.

This has no stimulus effect.

This usually means throwing good money after bad. GM looks to be declaring bankruptcy even after a significant bailout. Will the taxpayers recover their money?

Congress is currently creating a nation of Whinners (winners by whining). I need a bridge to my island in Alaska, boo-hoo boo-hoo. I need help for my town in Michigan hit by the auto downturn, boo-hoo boo-hoo. I made some bad investments, some sub-prime some not; I need help, boo-hoo boo-hoo. If you don't whine you don't get. Of course direct whining looks unseemly so you have to hire a silver-tongued lobbyist to rationalize the Congressman's position.

Use ultra Keynesian Fiscal Stimulus

That is: increase the deficit.

This may stimulate the economy although the past evidence on the matter is ambiguous.

Furthermore, the effect of such stimulus is a long time in coming. Deficit financed infrastructure requires design, engineering, planning, hiring before any significant monies find their way into the economy.

Often such rushed expenditures are associated with large cost overruns, financial abuse, and in retrospect would have been more productively spent elsewhere.

The worst part is that such expenditures appear to have no cost, and once on that slippery hill......

Use Galbraithian fiscal stimulus

That is: tax-and-spend to address the bias in the economy towards private expenditures. John Kenneth Galbraith coined the phrase: Private Affluence – Public Poverty.

His various arguments ring true on this matter. His Keynesian style policy also has a slight stimulus effect by taking a dollar from the consumer – only a portion of which is spent (the other part is saved) and letting the government spend the full dollar.

Unfortunately this argument overlooks the fact that if the consumer savings are not spent as I (investment) or G (government spending) then there will be a downward force on prices to bring things into balance.

All in all: not a bad theory to guide government expenditures but is of little or no help in a time of recession.

Fix the money supply at a constant growth rate

This Chicago School / Milton Freidman approach would take away the one government policy which has a chance to increase the value of assets via expansion of the money supply. Clearly markets whether free or not can get into serious trouble and continue worsening without some government action.

Lower Interest Rates Further

Forcing nominal rates below zero is not possible. But there should be no hesitation in forcing real interest rates below zero. Real interest rates are the nominal or actual rate adjusted for inflation. For example if the bank rate averages 3.5% over a period, and the CPI (or some other measure of inflation) is 4.5% over that same period, then the period specific real rate of interest is minus 1.0%.

Negative real rates have prevailed in the past and will do so in the future. The situation is fundamentally un-tenable in the sense that investors will only have to pay back less than the principal amount of their real loans and in the meantime find any investment which pays some sort of return. But the seeds of a recovery are planted.

Will this work in the present situation?: No. Already nominal rates are close to zero. Rates were lowered too slowly to have a significant effect. Now that we are caught in the liquidity trap, the only solution is pushing cash into the system via FOMC purchases.

The FOMC folks normally meet eight times a year. Lately they have been meeting every four weeks. Suggestion: meet every day. And if any member of the FOMC harrumph-harrumphs about what we really need to worry about is the growing inflationary pressures, nudge him aside.

Expand the FEDs Liquidization Program

Of course! Set up eleven FOMCs (the Federal Reserve Bank of New York implements the FOMC decisions) to match each of the Fed banks. Let them compete to see who can make the most profit for the government by buying oil, oil stocks, senior equities, senior bonds (private and government), and even some derivatives. No shorting directly or indirectly. Go long, be strong. Of course, they would not be credited with making a profit until they resold such assets back to the private sector in the good times.

The Future

When will the Great Recession of 09 end? Sometime in 2010 if expansionary monetary policy is pursued.

But it is difficult to gage this one. We are in the midst of a classic financial panic.

The strange thing is that there is absolutely no foundation for this panic. Workers were working and working productively. Costs were increasing but fundamentally because of galloping oil prices yet clearly the wheels were set in motion by these high prices to wean us off our dependence on oil. Technological advances were and are continuing apace and were and are continually finding their way into our mainstream consumption goods. Income and wealth were increasing around the globe with a corresponding growth in consumer demand.

Basically, we choked the golden goose with our anti-inflationary policies.

Knowledge of what is possible is the beginning of happiness. (George Santayana)

The day of free energy is fast approaching. George Bernard Shaw used to say that work is just moving stuff from one place to another. Of course there are workers needed to convince others to move the stuff from one place to another. Then there are those who finance such actions, taking a nice taste of the action all the while. Nonetheless, with cheap energy the job gets a lot easier.

Soon it will be become evident that governments can simply give away electrical energy, saving everyone a lot of distribution and collection costs. It will start on the freeways: embedded sensor/conductors will 'top up' vehicle batteries as they move long distances. It will soon become obvious that 'smarts' can be packaged with this distribution system. Initially long haul trucks will be 'robotically' driven in highway closure times, say between 1:00 am and 6:00 am. Soon someone will notice that accidents are not as prevalent as when humans are doing the job and the system will be extended to all intercity traffic. Next step?: the cities.

Free energy also alleviates the shortage of other commodities. With energy you can 'transmogrify' most anything into anything else.

And then there are the robots. It will soon be discovered that robots need not be built in the image of humans. Control robots, assigned to a human master, will pick-and-place sub-robots optimized to perform specific tasks as laid out by the master.

Technological advances in materials already are mind boggling. The world of designer materials is upon us. Strength of steel but flexible, transparent but conductive, and a variety of other very useful characteristics are being developed in materials that are designed from the atom up. If Mr. Robinson's business associate were alive today, he would counsel the daughter's boyfriend: one word – nanotechnology.

Advances in computing continue apace. Take a look at Intel's business plan. WOW! And quantum computing has a prospect of leaping us past Moore's Law.

All this is within the world of the possible. The technology is proven. What remains is the inevitable jockeying in the market as to which of the various competing, excellent, and workable, technologies is the best. Even though BETA was a huge advance over reel-to-reel, it lost out to VHS. Nobody wants to be stuck with a BETA capital cost.

With all the effort and money applied to pure, and to applied research, just imagine the un-imaginable advances to come. Another transistor. Another internet. We don't know what but we know it is coming.

As to basic safety for persons, and for commerce, we are entering a new world. It need not be a Big Brother world where everything/everybody is 'tracked'; it need only be trackable. Voice and video recording will be pervasive both in time and space. The government won't bother keeping track of you (may even be made illegal) but if a crime is committed the ubiquitous recordings will be able to track the criminal backwards and forwards in both time and space. This trend is well underway: consider the fact that most of London is under some security or traffic camera already. Add to that the development of face recognition algorithms for computers, and you have the seeds planted.

So the future is great, right? Wrong!

Big problem looming. How do we earn our incomes if basically everything is free? Will entertainers and engineers be rich and the rest of us poor and unemployable?

I think it is time to try to think out a new economics.

What we currently call greed may just be the amassing of stuff in order to be secure against the ravages that sweep through economic systems. We don't really want an infinite number of Chevy Malibu no matter how low the price.

What we all want is security, titillation, input, and companionship. That last one might be redundant to the others.

Also, while 'stuff' may well be virtually free in the future, we all have shortages that affect our consumption: space (an inability to consume more than one thing at the same place) and time (an inability to consume simultaneously).

Without suggesting how, a new theory of the 'distribution of not so scarce resources, amongst not so competing ends', should/could be developed.

We do have the seeds of a new economics.

If we don't do something, the coming good times could be really bad.

www.ingramcontent.com/pod-product-compliance
Lightning Source LLC
Chambersburg PA
CBHW081224170526

45165CB00009B/2947